T0165237

The String of Pearls

Miracles of the Dome of Creation

Don Lucas

WestBow
PRESS
A DIVISION OF THOMAS NELSON

WestBow Press books may be ordered through booksellers or by contacting:

WestBow Press
A Division of Thomas Nelson
1663 Liberty Drive
Bloomington, IN 47403
www.westbowpress.com
1-(866) 928-1240

Because of the dynamic nature of the Internet, any web addresses or links contained in this book may have changed since publication and may no longer be valid. The views expressed in this work are solely those of the author and do not necessarily reflect the views of the publisher, and the publisher hereby disclaims any responsibility for them.

Any people depicted in stock imagery provided by Thinkstock are models, and such images are being used for illustrative purposes only.

Certain stock imagery © Thinkstock.

ISBN: 978-1-4497-3225-7 (sc)
ISBN: 978-1-4497-3226-4 (hc)
ISBN: 978-1-4497-3224-0 (e)

Library of Congress Control Number: 2011962734

Printed in the United States of America

WestBow Press rev. date: 1/12/2012

Contents

Dedication and My Journal Prayer

I want to dedicate my journal first and foremost to my Special Angel Nina, Martine, her daughter Anne, Judy, Edwin, Clara, Elizabeth, Mary from Africa, Barbara, her daughter "THE WALKING MIRACLE" and of the more than 600 others all in Virginia and my loving brother Fabian in Ohio and especially to the inspirational driver and guide of this journal our creator GOD'S HOLY SPIRIT; additionally, I want to acknowledge the seven priests who believed me from my first disclosure of this miracle and continue to believe; Father Jack Fullen RIG, Bishop Zubik of Pittsburg, Father Daniel from Africa, Father Joseph, Father Wilson from Chicago but assigned to Nativity Parish, Father Bork and Father Murungi; who commented, "you look normal to me"; I am normal and my post-evidentiary effects you are about to read are proof of this fact; it definitely wasn't a dream or of my design; this evidence was given to me exclusively by God through HIS "Dome Of Creation". I acknowledge also the following individual to which I owe a great deal of gratitude.

Word processing: Anne

Prayer

Come HOLY SPIRIT enkindle in me the fire of your love for this journal and demonstrate to me and the entire world your awesome prayer power; YOU gifted to me on the very best day of my life, from YOUR Dome of Creation and the gates of hell shall not prevail against its success. AMEN!

Preface

Don's journal: A non-fictional chronological and complete eye witness testimony of my near-death/out of body experience and its post- evidentiary effects; another recipe for man's salvation as seen through the eyes of our creator GOD's HOLY SPIRIT and the mysterious, awesome power HE possesses. It is simply another tool in HIS arsenal to rescue our soul from Satan's grip; so we can return to our heavenly father and he can welcome us home with open arms and say to us, "come in my faithful servant and receive your reward prepared for you from the foundation of the world". I think it is appropriate for me to begin this journal by borrowing words from a popular song by Elvis Presley; one of my favorite artists. "Welcome to my world, won't you come on in; miracles I guess still happen now and then; step into my life; leave your world behind; welcome to my world, a world with you in mind." It's a world of truth, but more importantly of "PROOF OF LIFE AFTER LIFE." The following messages bear this out (no. 21 and no.22) since my 70th birthday in the year 2007, from GOD's HOLY SPIRIT: (30 Mar 10) Tuesday of HOLY week: I received a message (no.21) from the spirit at 3:00 p.m. this afternoon; I was in the process of beginning my 45th novena (Sign of 9's) meaning 9 days of prayer utilizing my mom's large rosary; given to me by my brother Fabian. It said, "use the journal for my father's glory; you have proof of "Life After Life"; I will guide you; do not be afraid.'

(11 Apr 10) Sunday: I received another message (no.22) from the spirit at 8:30 a.m. on this "Divine Mercy Sunday"; second Sunday of Easter as follows: "give the journal as a gift from my HOLY SPIRIT to the world; to demonstrate my spirits power and don't be concerned about Satan; I will neutralize him and the gates of hell will not prevail against this." I am a rescuer of souls, especially the lost ones, on what I call, an "M.M.A.S.", meaning a mission of mercy for all souls created by GOD; because I now know this is from GOD to all of you my readers and to the entire world. Because of near-death experience, I've decided to remove from my vocabulary two words, "believe" and "death"; they are superfluous. "Believe" now equals "know" and "death" equals, "passing on"; we will not

die, the only souls that will die, are those sentenced from GOD to hell for all eternity. Their chief punishment is not seeing their creator face to face and remaining in torment and complete darkness forever. It's theological and can be proven through my experience and millions of others, that we all have an immortal soul and an intellect (a power in the soul) with a free will (to do or not to do) endowed by our creator with his image and likeness were going to "pass on" from the material world to the immaterial word; were going to live FOREVER; I know I was close to heaven where I was given a little glimpse and returned to this world and my post-evidence is the proof. Recall from "Natural Theology"; whose premise is knowing GOD through nature by his effects (causes) in the world; the definition of a miracle; a sensible event outside the powers of all nature done by God alone and "the test of truth is the objective evidence" of course I will let you, my reader, ascertain whether this experience is a natural cause (caused by nature) or a supernatural cause by GOD and therefore a miracle? It's your prerogative, not mine. Throughout my journal a great deal of my testimony will be redundant; a technique I will use to over emphasize our creator GOD's supreme power. Remember also GOD is the Supreme Being who made all things; being immutable, meaning he can't change and he can't error; HE's omnipotent meaning HE's almighty. All powerful and he has omniscience, complete infinite knowledge and he also is a necessary being and an intelligent being, meaning he possesses a perfect communicable intellect; what an awesome GOD we have; we should all rejoice and thank HIM for all he has given and continues to give HIS "Agape", meaning, "perfect love" to HIS creation; enjoy this journal; a snippet of HIS love from our creator to me and now to you. This journal simply isn't a novel; it actually happened to me that wonderful January morning and is still happening as I deliver this message to you, from the HOLY SPIRIT, my advocate and guide here on earth. Please keep in mind reader that before you make that ultimate decision of my experience, as to being a miracle or not; there are "NO COINCIDENCES IN LIFE, ONLY STEPS IN GODS PLAN." I want to borrow words from another favorite song of mine and I hope you recall it too; "it is no secret what GOD can do, what HE's done for others HE'LL do for you; with arms wide open HE'LL pardon you, it is no secret what GOD can do", HE selected me and did it for me now he can do it for you; that's the message I want to send in this journal. I'm sure that whoever peruses this journal will receive a blessing of healing and inspirational power for both themselves and their families, from our heavenly father and I pray that their ultimate reward will be eternal life with him in heaven. AMEN, meaning, "so be it".

Abbreviations And Definitions

1. C= The number of possible combinations in the year 2007 (in this case)
2. Collinear= Lying on or passing through the same straight line (continuous function)
3. CPA= Civilian Prayer Answered or Criminal Prayer Answered depending on event characteristics
4. Delta's= The number of days (9) between significant events establishing the Sign of 9's
5. EWTN= Eternal World Television Network (channel 370 on Directv)
6. N= 365 days/year (2007 in this case)
7. NCIC= New Creature In CHRIST
8. NDE= Near-Death experience
9. P= The probability of occurrence of an event, equals one divided by C (as defined above) since C is in the denominator of this fraction, P will always equal ZERO, because it is a negative exponent, meaning, its power of 10 is always negative; thus its value=0
10. Pearl= A) precious gem or gift from the HOLY SPIRIT
    B) A metaphor or an analogy for "Little Kingdoms of heaven", representing a math coordinate (X,Y) of a point on The String or Straight Line (continuous function) a direct link to my NDE
11. Plane Of The Pearls= A rectangle whose height dimension is equal to the number of years of my life and whose length dimension is eternity or infinity as a limit and it contains the miracle equation $Y1=70$, whose limit approaches infinity also because it lies within the plane.
12. Post-Evidentiary effects= After evidence in proving the miracle

13. R= The number of significant dates, pearls, points or solutions to the math equation in this case a straight line or string
14. RIG= Rest in Glory
15. WPA= War Prayer Answered
16. Xlation= Translation
17. Xferred= Transferred

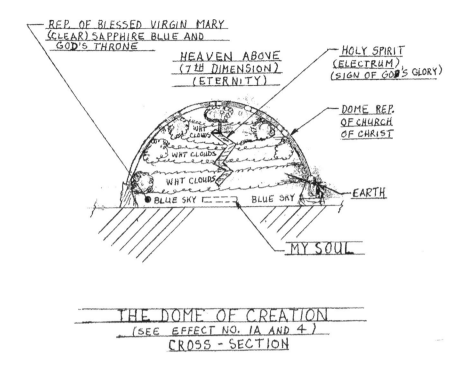

REP. OF BLESSED VIRGIN MARY (CLEAR) SAPPHIRE BLUE AND GOD'S THRONE

HEAVEN ABOVE (7TH DIMENSION) (ETERNITY)

HOLY SPIRIT (ELECTRUM) (SIGN OF GOD'S GLORY)

DOME REP. OF CHURCH OF CHRIST

WHT CLOUDS

WHT CLOUDS

WHT CLOUDS

BLUE SKY   BLUE SKY

EARTH

MY SOUL

THE DOME OF CREATION
(SEE EFFECT NO. 1A AND 4)
CROSS - SECTION

1. Change of Journal Title

(01 Aug 10) Sunday (out of seq.): Your probably wondering why I would begin my journal fast forwarding to (2010) when my near-death experience, the main thrust of this journey through time, occurred in 2007; my reason; I received one of the most important messages (my 24th) from the spirit this morning at 5:03 a.m. I was told to change the title of the journal; you can imagine my distress and wonderment at this last stage of the final draft but I could not ignore the preceding joy I experienced, as I received in all previous messages; that portion of the title, meaning; "the straight line miracles," is now called "The String Of Pearls Miracles"; for each post-evidentiary effect is analogous to the pearl, a precious gem; a gift from the HOLY SPIRIT, I received during the Dome experience additionally, all the pearls on the string are in intimate contact with each other depicting our relationship with each other, as children of GOD and the entire world; all linking to that first pearl on the string, my near-death experience in a straight path, in this case the straight line miracle equation (see graphic effect

no.30) an analogy between the pearl, our immortal soul and the track were on to infinity (eternity with GOD); remember GOD says in his word, "the path to destruction is wide and many will follow that path, but the road to everlasting life is very narrow and relatively few will pass through the narrow gate of heaven;" meaning all pearls involving GODS children, are special gifts from heaven their souls must return through :the narrow gate:; the main purpose for "the String Of Pearls"; also the kingdom of heaven is compared to the pearl in GODS parable; as I recall the following verse (Matthew 13:45); "the kingdom of heaven is like a merchant searching for fine pearls; when he finds a pearl of great price, he goes and sells all that he has and buys it," ; as a result, I must honor this request of my advocate and guide, the HOLY SPIRIT.

1A. Near- Death Experience (Sign of 9's Begins)

(09 Jan 07) Tuesday: I was alone at 7:00 a.m. and was sitting on the edge of my bed fully aware and awake at the time ready to begin my day. All of a sudden I thought I was outside in the grass looking up, but I was someplace I hadn't been before. I encountered a magnificently, beautiful, perfectly symmetrical, marvelous Dome above me, with rings of concentric, dazzling, billowing, white clouds and the most beautiful sky between each ring of clouds I had ever seen, likened to a precious clear blue sapphire stone; the clouds rose to the top of the Dome, and at the apex, I saw what resembled an ornament suspended from the smallest white cloud it was shaped like a zig-zag bolt of stationary lightning with speckled gold surface, about 10 feet long; it was eminating soft light; the Dome approached me and seemed to pass through me, piercing me with the ornament. I was startled, all through the very short elapsed time I was experiencing waves of total overwhelming joy permeating every fiber of my being. I knew immediately I had an out-of-body experience and my soul had returned to my body at the speed of light. In the exact position still on the edge of my bed, my only response was WOW! What was that? (My 1st miracle) and possibly my 1st angel visit (see effect no. 37). This date produces the 1st pearl (see graphics effect no. 30). The following results of what had turned out to be "the very best day of my life of 69.8 years" is this, I received from the HOLY SPIRIT charisms,

meaning, spiritual gifts (special graces, deep faith, speaking in tongue and miracles); (refer to effect no. 28). These are the first fruits of the spirit my creator GOD has blessed me with. What I have previously called and will emphasize post evidentiary effects, precious gems or pearls, events, points or solutions to my miracle equation (see graphic effect no. 30) all of these are metaphors or signs, even the numbers in mathematical calculations, that GOD is using freely and mysteriously demonstrating, not only to me, but to the whole world, HIS perfect love and only a glimpse of the tremendous power he possesses and my readers, even as I write these words today, I can honestly say, "GOD isn't through with me yet", as of August 2010. Every day of my life I will give thanks to my heavenly father for these amazing gifts and experiences by attending daily mass (one of my transformations) which I have never done before in my entire life until now, diligently praying novenas (9 days of prayer, my "sign of 9's" which began on this day) (09 Jan 07) my near-death experience and keeping a prayer list, praying for friends and family, the healing of the sick, bringing criminals, both civilian (CPA) and war types (WPA) to justice, and peace in our world; I am dedicating this journal to that end. After further investigation, the following is my own observance. I'm sure my soul when it left my body for that infinitesimal period of time, didn't pass through walls and because I know that my soul was headed for heaven that morning, but GOD was returning me to earth as HIS messenger, so it necessitated HIM to put the Dome in my path; dimension wise, we have length, width, depth, space and time. Those are the five dimensions we experience in the world. The sixth dimension cannot be used, because per the Book of Revelation in the bible; the no. 6 equals imperfection and is usually attributable to Satan; such as (666). I invoked the spirit on this fact for three years, and I know I'm correct   when I say, "the 7th dimension is eternity; because the no.7 equals, TOTALITY OF PERFECTION and GOD is in zero time; thus another reason for the "7" appearing on my upper right arm (see effect no. 37). Eternity is where I encountered the "Dome of Creation." GOD only let me observe what HE wanted, then returned my soul to my body; still in the identical position from which it departed (eyes opened and sitting on the edge of my bed) one nanosecond before similar to the elapsed time of the shutter speed of a camera, the blink of an eye or the flick of a light switch.

1B. Explanation By Expert Father Jack Fullen

(07 May 10) Friday (Out of Seq.): This turned out to be one of the saddest days of my life, on one hand because of GOD's calling of Father Jack Fullen, who had given me the correct explanation of my encounter with 'the Dome of Creation," but on the other hand the no. 7 (see effect no. 37) indicated he passed on TOTALITY OF PERFECTION, which he so richly deserved. God rewarded him with this great distinction. I want to flash back to the first time I met him and under what circumstances because if we never met, I would have considered my entire experience just a dream and this journey would have ended (07 April 07) Saturday. It began on this April day after I attended the Vigil mass where the gospel reading was from Genesis; "the Dome of the Sky" he had just completed. I first noticed my opportunity to meet him and introduce myself as he was getting into his vehicle telling him of an encounter with a Dome, and the overwhelming joy I experienced throughout the marvelous infinitesimal moment of earthly time, before I could describe the characteristics of this Dome, he interrupted me by stating this fact, "I know exactly where you were." Of course I couldn't believe my ears. I was startled. He said, "I was in the presence of representations of heavenly manifestations" and began to give me the following explanation. "the Dome itself represented the church of CHRIST; the blue sky in between the rings of dazzling white clouds represented the Virgin Mary and God's sapphire blue throne and I asked him "what was the centerpiece suspended from the apex from the Dome eminating soft light, and having a beautiful gold appearance, which I later discovered was actually ELECTRUM a sign of God's glory, his answer was, "it was her spouse, the HOLY SPIRIT and the clouds were what she stands on when she appears on earth, because in all of her apparitions at Fatima, Lourdes, Megigore and other sightings, she never touches the corrupt soil of earth" he continued by saying, "when the Dome approached me and the centerpiece pierced my soul I received the HOLY SPIRIT, which gave me a mission to fulfill from my heavenly father, while immediately receiving complete healing and forgiveness of my past life and all

transgressions against him thus I was recreated and returned to my body on earth to become a modern day apostle, because when we are baptized (baptism means, "to be sent") we put on GOD's heavenly garment to go out to the world to save as many souls for HIM as possible, while keeping Satan at bay. I will miss Father Jack dearly. He was assigned to me as my spiritual advisor, but the HOLY SPIRIT led me away from St. Raymonds at the end of June 2007. I later discovered that Father Jack Fullen was an expert in near-death, out-of-body experiences all over the world. Imagine, I was led to him by the HOLY SPIRIT himself. On Wednesday (12 may 10), Father Jack was laid to rest (Sign of the 12's) (see effect no. 9), we will all miss him and the way he touched the people who were lucky to have been in his presence. This date was "the Vigil of the memorial of our lady of Fatima" AMEN.

Father Jack can now be considered and utilized as my patron saint and along with the HOLY SPIRIT advocates of this journal.

2.   Margot (Similar Near-Death Experience)

(16 Apr 07) Tuesday: I had been a member of St. Raymonds Parish since January and this date I met, probably the second most important person in my life (the first would be Father Jack Fullen). I was turning to my left, after mass, towards the parking lot when the spirit turned me towards a wonderful lady on my right in the vestibule of the church. I introduced myself to Mary (same name as my mother who passed on in 1988). After relating my near-death experience to her she told me to contact her mother Margot in Detroit, Michigan because she also had a near-death experience two years ago. I contacted her mother (12 May 07), this entire state I was going through and confusion relating my near-death experience delayed our communication with each other. Margot said this, "I was clinically pronounced dead in my hospital bed with all my children (she had seven children including Mary around my bed praying for the repose of my soul) I was aware of my soul leaving my body and in the presence of a blinding white light." I asked if she seen a dome and she said "the light was too bright" but she then heard a voice (I told her I didn't) she immediately knew it was the Lord's voice. He told her, "it wasn't her time yet and HE would lead her to what she's doing today; working seven

days per week on her rosary workshop while drawing people closer to GOD. Her new vocation, for the last several years now is found on her website (www.rosaryworkshop.com) we met in June 2007 in Virginia. She told me to document all my events in 2007 and beyond. She said, "GOD will be teasing me in the future." She was absolutely correct as I was to discover on my journey through time; thus my journal is born.

3.   Corroboration

(07 Apr 07) Saturday (Easter Vigil) (out of seq.): This dates event leads to total corroboration along with (see effects no. 1B meeting Father Jack Fullen for the first time) as follows: Easter Vigil Mass, Genesis readings at the gospel part of the mass referring to verse 1-20 ("the dome of the sky") and the only bible with the illustration you'll ever find in the world now infamous and ultimately important in my near-death experience; the Dome of creation" and of course, last but not least Margot's account of her near-death experience.

4.   Miracle Bible no. 611, Discovery of

(28 Apr 07) Saturday: This date is ultimately the third most important day of my life, because it produces my second miracle (possibly a visit from my second angel) (see effect no. 37) as follows: I had been discussing my near-death experience with my brother Fabian in Ohio from the beginning, so I visited him this weekend and encountered skepticism galore; dismissing my near-death experience as only a dream my brother Fabian said "let's go research your dome." I said, "where do we go" he suggested a book store in the mall I said, "which one" to which he replied, "Barnes and Noble." So we did. We were standing between two upright racks of different types of bibles when I turned to my right and a beautiful tan covered bible with a gold cross was exactly at my eye level so I removed it from the shelf and opened it to Genesis. It was "The new American Bible Saint Joseph Edition", a catholic type no. 611. As I looked at page 4 and an adjacent page, my brother Fabian behind me almost collapsed, for there we discovered the actual and only illustration in the world of my identical recall of my near-death experience; "The Dome of Creation" he said, "he

wanted to purchase it" since he now believes and I asked the clerk if there were any more available. He said, "this was the only bible of this type in the store." VOILA! The HOLY SPIRIT must have led us to this only bible; I asked the clerk, "to order me one and ship it to Virginia." As my brother bought this one, he complied and two weeks later I would receive my bible by

mail. Remember we must fast forward to effect no. 39 (06 Feb 09) to discover (pearl no. 2) which contributes to the second miracle and because it falls on a Tuesday exactly on the straight line miracle equation (Y1=70) (see graphic effect no. 30). I discovered no. 611 bible was now for sale at Nativity. Where I am to this day, since (11 Oct 07) (see effect no. 37 and 58). The date I became a member of Nativity Parish in Burke, Virginia.

5.   My 70th Birthday (Message no.1) (Spirit Prompt)

(22 May 07) Tuesday: my 70th birthday; PROMPT FROM SPIRIT to attend my first R.C.I.A. class meaning (Rite of Christian Initiation for adults) (starting same day).

6.   'Satan Opposite Jesus'

(From Jan to May): Periodic waking between 3 and 4 a.m. (Devils Hour according to Father Jack Fullen) praying and neutralizing Satan; because he said, "Devil is tormenting someone at this hour and prayer needed immediately. Note: father Jack Fullen said Satan is opposite of Jesus because Jesus died at 3 p.m. in the afternoon and Satan since he is opposite of Jesus, he does his best work between 3 and 4 a.m. in the morning. Additionally, if you wake during the Devil's Hour you should pray to neutralize him as Father Jack instructed me to do.

7.   Reconciliation 1,2,3 (Message no. 2) (Spirit Prompt)

(08 Jun 07) Friday: PROMPT FROM SPIRIT; my reconciliation (with Ann, Walt and Jim) neighbors.

8. Contact no.1 By Phone With My Brother William (Message no. 3) (Spirit Prompt)---

    (15 Jun 07) Friday: PROMPT FROM SPIRIT; my first telephone conversation with William (my close brother) the start of reconciliation and our future contacts by phone.

9. Mom's Prayer (Message no. 4) (Spirit Prompt)

    (18 Jun 07) Monday: PROMPT FROM SPIRIT; composing of Mom's prayer. The following is an excerpt from the more than two thousand prayers delivered to the world. My mother gave me this prayer at age sixteen and I am now 70. Please accept and learn this prayer and share it with your friends and neighbors. Say it every day, as I have done since it was given to me. Recently, (five months ago) one beautiful January morning (09 Jan 07) (note: Sign of 9's begins), I had a true out of body near-death experience. God changed my life that day and I want to share that joy with the world. HE can do the same for you if you ask HIM. My experience proves HE loves us, for we are HIS children and HE protects us from the evil in this world. Remember, God said, "you will have trouble in the world, but I have conquered the world." I call this letter, "GOD's CHAIN" because I believe HE wants it to "wrap around the world" in eighty days or fewer. Let's do God's work for a change and send HIS message to all people especially young people, regardless of skin color, religious affiliation, or nationality. HE LOVES US ALL. After all, isn't this a love letter from man to God, thanking him for the many blessings he has bestowed on us? Feel free to contact me and learn more about my encounter with "The Dome of Creation" and seven miracles (in my 70th year) I received in 2007, now nine miracles as of 2010. Thank you for listening. Don't break one link of the chain. GOD BLESS YOU. The following facts are important here [note: the power of the HOLY SPIRIT "GOD"; he used numbers (math); my expertise]. The graphics effect no. 30 bears this out. Sign of the 7's: because the number 7 appeared on my right arm for seven days (see effect no. 37).

    1. 7= The "TOTALITY OF PERFECTION" per Revelation in my no. 611 miracle bible.

2. 7= Spirits of GODS (Angels) messengers of God around his throne per revelation in no. 611 miracle bible.
3. 7= The number of stars of David.
4. GOD rested on the 7th day of creation.
5. 7= Miracles of my Dome in 2007 in my 70th year.
6. 7= Gifts of the HOLY SPIRIT
7. 7= Works of mercy
8. 7= Sacraments in the church
9. 7= The exact number of the priests who believed me and still do four years later.

Sign of the 9's

1. 9= Novena (9 days of prayer)
2. 9= Days between significant supernatural events
3. I learned Barbara healed of cancer (effect no. 38) on (09 Oct 09)
4. 911 vs. 611 "Satan opposite JESUS"
5. My near-death experience date (09 Jan 07)
6. 9th hour is when JESUS died
7. 9= Choirs of angels

Sign of the 12's

1. 12= number of apostles
2. 12= tribes of Israel
3. 12= Rosary beads per mystery
4. 12= stars around the Blessed Virgin Mary
5. 12 years of my prayer for reconciliation with GOD
6. The following is the complete "Our Savior's Letter"

This prayer was found on the grave of our lord Jesus Christ in the year 1505 and was sent by the Pope to the emperor Charles as he was going to the battle, for safety. They who shall repeat this prayer every day or hear it repeated, or keep it about them, shall never die a sudden death, nor be drowned in water nor shall poison take any effect on them, nor shall they fall into the hands of their enemies, nor be burned in fire, nor shall they be overpowered in battle; and in being read over a woman in labor she shall be protected from misfortunes; and if anyone of you see anyone in fits, lay them on their right rise, and they will stand up and thank you; and he that shall laugh at it shall suffer, and they shall distribute it from door to door shall be blessed by the LORD. Believe it for certain that which is written here is true as the Holy Evangelists. They who shall keep it about them shall have three warning days before death.

PRAYER

O Adorable Lord and Savior JESUS CHRIST dying on the cross for our lives, O Holy Cross of CHRIST, ward off from me all sharp repeating words; O Holy Cross of CHRIST, protect me from my enemies; O Holy Cross of CHRIST, ward off from me a sudden and unprovided death and give me a life eternal.

In the honor of our Lord and savior Jesus Christ and in honor of His Sacred Passion, in Honor of his Glorious Resurrection and Ascension, by which HE opened the right way to heaven for me, as true as JESUS CHRIST was born in a stable, as true as three kings brought offerings there to JESUS on the 13th day; as true as JESUS was crucified on Good Friday; as true as HE ascended into Heaven, so the power of JESUS will shield me from my enemies, visible and invisible, now and forever.

To Thee, O Lord JESUS CHRIST, to thee I offer my spirit. JESUS have mercy on me. Mary and Joseph, pray for me. Through Nicodemus and Joseph who took Jesus down from the cross and buried HIM. O Lord JESUS, through our anguish and passion for Thy Son, have mercy on my poor soul when parting out of this world. JESUS give me grace that I may carry my cross patiently without dread and fear and without complaint, that through Thy sufferings I may escape all danger, now and forever and ever. AMEN!

10.   Acceptance of Mom's Prayer

(22 Jun 07) Friday: Start of around the world universal acceptance of Mom's prayer.

11.   Satan's First Attack

(25 Jun 07) Monday: Asked to sign written agreement by pastor at St. Raymond's; six months after joining church on Christmas day (25 Dec 06); I left R.C.I.A. I believe this to be Satan's first attack

to stop what I was accomplishing. The spirit led me away from this church. (Note: see my 2nd attack by Satan, effect no. 55)

12. HOLY SPIRIT Pamphlet Discovery (Message no.5) (Spirit Prompt)

(28 Jun 07) Thursday: PROMPT FROM SPIRIT; Started attending 9 a.m. mass at St. Bernadettes; was led to rack of pamphlets in vestibule of church; this is considered my third miracle or visit from my third Angel (see effect no. 37) when I selected HOLY SPIRIT type and sent to my brother Fabian in Ohio, without looking at the publishing date (June 1995) there were 25 pamphlets at the time and 24 were left. I received an angry phone call from Fabian about the date of the pamphlet, he said "why did you send me a pamphlet dated 1995, did you look at the back of the pamphlet?" and I said "no, I didn't" and he said "flip the pamphlet over and look at the imprimatur date (10 Apr 95). This is significant because I remembered that only sixteen days later (26 Apr 95) I started what turned out to be a 12 year reconciliation prayer with GOD and HE answered this prayer with my near-death experience (09 Jan 07) note: this is the first Sign of 9's delta (9 days between effect no. 12 and 13). The pamphlet whose title is, "Who Is The HOLY SPIRIT" and links to my near-death experience directly, because of the two dates (10 Apr 95) and (26 Apr 95), (the beginning of my 12 year reconciliation prayer, mentioned above) and also due to my being led to it on (28 Jun 07) falls on a Thursday, now can be considered my third miracle, third pearl, point, or solution to (Y1=70) (see graphic callouts no. 12 and effect no. 30 miracle calendar). I'm unable to use another writer's work, for I would be plagiarizing that pamphlet. I will only use God's word to support my claim and I quote, "the wind blows where it wills and you can hear the sound it makes, but you do not know where it comes from or where it goes" unquote, that it's analogous to the HOLY SPIRIT; additionally, the spirit is invisible and one must examine its post-evidentiary effects, as I do in this journal to detect its spiritual presence, in "our world."

13. Lou's Demise (sign of 9's, Delta no. 1)

(07 Jul 07) Saturday: PROMPT FROM SPIRIT concerning this time my brother Fabian, he was in Ohio and received this prompt

to visit his close cousin Lou who was in a coma in a hospice for about a year without talking. Fabian arrived and Lou immediately began speaking to him for three and a half hours after waking immediately from the coma and said the following as he was turning from the wall where he had been the whole time "Fabian, I knew you'd come", as he walked in the room with Lou's two grown children crying at his bedside. They were happy to see their father come out of the coma. Fabian left for home after Lou went back into his medical stupor and I found out later by a phone call from my brother that after my brother left Lou passed on (12 Jul 07) Thursday morning 2 a.m. (Rest In Glory).

14.   Similar Near-Death Experience (TV program)

(26 Jul 07) Thursday: I was drawn to watch the morning show about two people with similar near-death experiences to mine and Margot (Mary's mom) (see effect no. 2).

15.   Text Book Link With My Near-Death Experience

(31 Jul 07) Tuesday: I found no. 611 bible now considered our miracle bible (Fabian and I) as item three listed for sale on the inside rear cover of "the Saint Joseph Baltimore Catechism" (one of three required textbooks in R.C.I.A.) given to me on my birthday on my first day of class. (see graphic effect no. 30)

16.   My conversion With GOD/Church, Verified

(31 Jul 07) Tuesday: My conversion (same as all conversions) related in green reference book (paragraphs 1445, 1448-1458) another required textbook for R.C.I.A. titled "Catechism of Catholic Church, 2nd Edition." Note: this is the second Sign of 9's delta (9 days between effect no. 16 and 18 my fourth miracle)

17.   Phone Contact With Bob Accepted

(07 Aug 07) Tuesday: I wasn't supposed to contact any parishioner at St. Raymond's I had to contact Bob to get three books for Fabian. He accepted my call and told me about "The catholic Shop in Centreville." I had two books, "Faith Explained" and 'Saint

Joseph Baltimore Catechism." I purchased them and mailed them to my brother Fabian.

18.   Joy Experienced no. 2, Link With Dome (sign of 9's Delta no. 2)

(09 Aug 07) Thursday: As mentioned above this is the main portion of the second delta mentioned about (Sign of 9's). this becomes my fourth miracle or fourth Angel visit exactly seven months ("7" meaning the TOTALITY OF PERFECTION) (see effect no. 37) occurring in this manner: while awake and standing at my bed, an identical joy filled my body for 20 seconds (same as the first miracle in January my near-death experience). I felt another presence in the room so I reached for the light switch and no one was there and the joy left me. I knew this must have been the spirit as before because of the overwhelming joy I experienced.

19.   Why Near-Death Experience Occurs Today

(09 Aug 07) Thursday: I noticed that page 259 of the green reference book mentioned above on effect no. 16 paragraph 994 referred to, "some dead will be raised in our present days", if we received the Eucharist, JESUS pledges this. Note: I know this refers to GOD allowing near-death and out-of-body experience today.

20.   Attendance of 100 Daily Masses (Spirit Led)

(15 Aug 07) Wednesday: Note: 100 daily masses I attended since January miracle. This date is the Assumption of our Blessed Mother (Mary) into heaven. (Note: I never went to daily mass in my life).

21.   My Cousin Judy Believes (She Distributes Moms Prayer)

(16 Aug 07) Thursday: I sent my cousin Judy Christy in California; skeptic at first, but after seeing evidence, now believes and is now distributing "MOM's prayer", by E-mail around the world; China, Iraq, France, Germany, etc.

22.   My Investigation of Remaining Holy Spirit Pamphlets (Message no. 6)

(17 Aug 07) Friday: PROMPT FROM SPIRIT: to check the rack at St. Bernadettes; I was led to Jennifer (similar out of body experience) result; no more pamphlets in rack (see effect no. 12) and further no "Catholic update types." Note: This is the day I closely examined the one I had, finding the earliest date was (10 Apr 95).

23.   Margot's 75th Birthday Links To My Near-Death Experience

(19 Aug 07) Sunday: I met Mary again and told her about my fourth miracle on (09 Aug 07). She said "WOW"! that was Margot's 75th birthday (her mother). Note: she was the one who also had a near-death experience (see effect no. 2).

24.   Former Wife Telcon (Reconciliation no. 4) (Sign of 9's)

(09 Sept 07) Sunday: My former wife called. First time in 15 years, on one month exactly after fourth miracle' said "she doesn't hate me"; we talked for two hours with no negative comments (note: this is my fourth reconciliation).

25.   Reconciliation no. 5 With My Brother William

(27 Sept 07) Thursday: I visited my oldest brother William at a nursing home at 8:30 p.m. we watched Ohio state and Minnesota football game first half, I did return on the 29th of Sept at 9:30 p.m. Saturday, he was very happy to see me again and we talked about old times. This was the fifth reconciliation because this was my first meeting him in 16 years. Note: this is the same date as Jim Rost the veteran from Iraq who had also a near-death experience. (See effect no. 43).

26.   Reconciliations no. 6 and no. 7 (2007) (Message no. 7) (Spirit prompt)

(29 Sept 07) Saturday: I reconciled with Sue and Richard at mom's house. I hadn't seen them in five years and they were very happy to see me. This was precipitated by PROMPT FROM SPIRIT. This is considered my sixth and seventh reconciliation. Note: this Dome

has turned out to be a reconciliation Dome, because I had a grand total of seven reconciliations in the year 2007 (my 70th year) the no, 7 representing TOTALITY OF PERFECTION (see effect no. 37) therefore, the Dome also represents perfection because GOD is the only perfect being in existence. The only conclusion to be drawn for the cause of my near-death experience can only be our creator GOD HIMSELF. There is no other sufficient explanation. AMEN!

27.   Meeting no.1 With Father Daniel (HE BELIEVES) (Message no. 8) (Spirit Prompt)--

(21 Oct 07) Sunday: PROMPT FROM SPIRIT to disclose fully with father Daniel (visiting Nativity from Africa) with Bishop George. Father believed in this miracle and me and asked me to "PRAY FOR HIM" after he blessed me and then he returned to Africa the next day.

28.   Joy Experienced no. 3, Link With Dome (Message no. 9, no. 10, no. 11) (Spirit Prompt)--

(20 Nov 07) Tuesday: my fifth miracle or fifth angel visit (see effect no. 37) was at 2:42 a.m. this morning when I woke up fully aware of the identical joy I experienced in the dome of waves passing through my body from head to toe. I knew then this was the spirit as before. The joyful waves lasted while I was under the covers until 3 a.m. (Devil's Hour). I received three messages this time as follows: no.1 Fabian be careful Satan is in your corner this refers to my brother having marital problems. No. 2 page 485 of green reference book, remember this was the "New Catholic Catechism" referred to (see effect no. 16) "some Christians" will receive charisms, meaning, "special grace's, gifts of miracles or tongues". No. 3 Richard Bracken "be ready" (my brothers friend a surgeon who lived across the street); I had been praying for him.

29.   Verify (sign of 9's) Link With Dome

(22 Jan 08) Tuesday: This date happens to be the thirty fifth anniversary of "Roe v. Wade" and the "March for life." This is the ninth month and on the same day Tuesday as my 70th birthday (22 May 07) therefore, the 9's are connected to the "Miracles of the Dome."

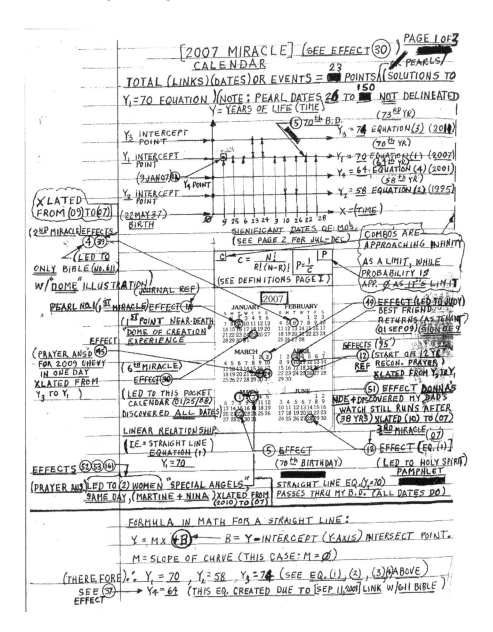

NOTE: THE (7TH MIRACLE) EFFECT (31) [PEARL NO. 7], OF THE JOURNAL; THE BLUE COLOR OF THE SASH OF (B.V.M) (BLESSED VIRGIN MARY) STATUE MATCHING THE BLUE SKY IN THE DOME, IS STILL VALID; IT OCCURRED IN (08), BUT BY XLATION PROCESS IT CAN BE (07).

NOTE: JIM ROST SAYS, "BLUE SASH" MATCHES BLUE DECORATION ON MARINE UNIFORM

(14) EFFECT [DRAWN TO WATCH MORNING SHOW W/SIMILAR EXP.(2)]

(13) EFFECT (MY COUSIN LOU'S PASSING) BACK TO BACK W/(14)

EFFECT (15) (MIRACLE BIBLE FOR SALE IN REQ'D TEXT BOOK)

EFFECT (37) LINK W/9/11 N.Y. XLATED FROM (01) TO (07)

EFFECTS

(25) (43)

(JIM ROST) SIMILAR EXP. IN IRAQ (NEAR-DEATH)

(MY 5TH RECON. W/ MY BRO. BILL BEFORE HE PASSED)

EFFECT (18) (2ND JOY EXP. AFTER DOME 4TH MIRACLE) BACK TO BACK W/(1A)

(43) EFFECT (FIRST MET JIM ROST XLATED (SIMILAR EXP. FROM (09) (BACK TO BACK W/(30) TO (07)

(38) EFFECT (BARBARA'S HEALED) XLATED (OF CANCER (2YR) FROM 09 (PRAYER ANS'D TO (07) 8TH MIRACLE ALSO (SIGN OF 9's (22 OCT 09

(TAN COVER)
(42) EFFECT (COLOR MATCH, NO. 611 BIBLE W/ RAISED PORTION OF THE NO. 7 ON MY ARM BACK TO BACK W/(5)

9TH MIRACLE XLATED FROM (09) TO (07) AFTER READING NO. 611 BIBLE ON A PROMPT FROM SPIRIT

(28) EFFECT (3RD JOY EXP. AFTER "DOME") (5TH MIRACLE)

[2007]

JULY
S M T W T F S
1 2 3 4 5 6 7
8 9 10 11 12 13 14
15 16 17 18 19 20 21
22 23 24 25 26 27 28
29 30 31

AUGUST
S M T W T F S
1 2 3 4
5 6 7 8 9 10 11
12 13 14 15 16 17 18
19 20 21 22 23 24 25
26 27 28 29 30 31

SEPTEMBER
S M T W T F S
1
2 3 4 5 6 7 8
9 10 11 12 13 14 15
16 17 18 19 20 21 22
23 24 25 26 27 28 29
30

OCTOBER
S M T W T F S
1 2 3 4 5 6
7 8 9 10 11 12 13
14 15 16 17 18 19 20
21 22 23 24 25 26 27
28 29 30 31

NOVEMBER
S M T W T F S
1 2 3
4 5 6 7 8 9 10
11 12 13 14 15 16 17
18 19 20 21 22 23 24
25 26 27 28 29 30

DECEMBER
S M T W T F S
1
2 3 4 5 6 7 8
9 10 11 12 13 14 15
16 17 18 19 20 21 22
23 24 25 26 27 28 29
30 31

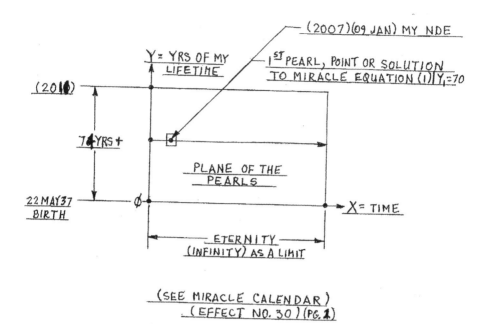

(SEE MIRACLE CALENDAR)
(EFFECT NO. 30) (PG. 1)

(25 Jan 08) Friday: PROMPT FROM SPIRIT; this was to be the sixth miracle or sixth Angel visit (see effect no. 37) for me to check the pocket calendar on my coffee table, it was a wallet size calendar 2007. I had circled with ball point pen all miracle dates and my cousin Lou's passing date (12 Jul 07) and my birthday (22 May). I noticed that all dates (pearl's, points or solutions) coincide with each other meaning, they were linear [straight line continuous function (note: this date is, "the conversion of St. Paul")]; I made an engineering model of my calendar by zeroxing each side back to back. I installed a needle through January ninth (first dome miracle) and all other dates; the needle representing the miracle equation, of course, passed through in a straight line, therefore all four dates are connected to my birthday the fifth date. I calculated this probability of occurrence; one chance in 5.3×10^{10}. this indicates or suggests supernatural cause, not natural. (Sign of 9's delta no. 3 between effect no. 30 and 31). In my analysis of the events indicated on the 2007 miracle calendar, I noticed what can be considered another (sign of 9's), which began on my near-death experience date (09 Jan 07) the crux date of this journey; at least (9 of 23 points or pearls) are on the straight line miracle equation

and can be considered true miracles reiterating as follows:

Miracle no. 1 (Pearl no. 1) effect no. 1A (09 Jan 07) Tuesday: Near-death of out body encounter with "Dome of Creation"

Miracle no. 2 (Pearl no. 2) effect no. 4 (06 Feb 09) Tuesday: Led for 2nd time to only miracle bible no. 611 with the Dome illustration (now at Nativity where I was led)

Miracle no. 3 (Pearl no. 3) effect no. 12 (28 Jun 07) Thursday: Led to, "who is the HOLY SPIRIT" pamphlet and its 1995 link to me

Miracle no. 4 (Pearl no. 4) effect no. 18 (09 Aug 07) Thursday: My 2nd overwhelming joy experience since (Jan 07) "Dome"

Miracle no. 5 (Pearl no. 5) effect no. 28 (20 Nov 07) Tuesday: My 3rd overwhelming joy experience and increased elapsed time since the "Dome"

Miracle no. 6 (Pearl no. 6) effect no. 30 (25 Jan 08) Friday (translated from 2008 to 2007 is now on a Thursday): I was led to this 2007 pocket calendar and discovered the linear relationship with all dates, pearls, points or solutions to miracle equation (Y1=70)

Miracle no. 7 (Pearl no. 7) effect no. 31 (03 Feb 08) Sunday: I was led to the discovery of the "Blessed Virgin Mary's statue of Lourdes"; blue-sash match with blue sky in the Dome. (see note on page 17 of effect no. 30)

Miracle no. 8 (Pearl no. 8) effect no. 38 (09 Oct 09) Monday (translated from 2009 to 2007 is now on a Tuesday): Mary's daughter Barbara completely healed of cancer; our answer to a two year prayer; she was given six months to live in 2007 (note: this is also the Sign of 9's

Miracle no. 9 (Pearl no. 9) effect no. 42 (25 Dec 09) Friday (translated from 2009 to 2007 is now on a Tuesday): the no. 7 on my arm (raised portion) was a perfect match with the tan cover of miracle bible no. 611

31.   Eternal World TV (EWTN) Link With Dome (Sign of 9's Delta no. 3) (Message no. 13) (Spirit Prompt)

(03 Feb 08) Sunday: PROMPT FROM SPIRIT to watch Eternal World Television Network (EWTN) channel 370 and the daily mass of Angels, on my re-installment of Directv (DTV); Sermon

was about 'Our Lady of Lourdes" (11 Feb 08); 150th anniversary of St. Bernadette; I noticed when the camera panned to Statue of Lourdes; a sapphire blue sash on the Blessed Virgin Mary statue is identical to the sapphire blue sky I encountered on (09 Jan 07) Dome. This becomes my 7th miracle or 7th angel visit (see effect no. 37); the sash is an upside down "V" shaped; draped from her waist toward the hem of her dress, inside her white veil; I was led to this event which constitutes the no. 7 miracle.

32.   Richard's Demise (Sign of 9's, Delta no. 4)

(08 Mar 08) Saturday: Dr. Richard Bracken passed on (Rest In Glory) Dick was 65 years old (Sign of 9's delta no. 4 effect no. 32 and 33) (Nine days between these two effects)

33.   William's Demise (Sign of 9's, Delta no. 4)

(16 Mar 08) Sunday (Palm Sunday): My beloved brother William passed on at 3:55 p.m. (Rest In Glory) he was 80 years old. (Note: I know Richard and William went immediately to heaven, because they received, "The Last Rites Sacrament of the Anointing of the Sick"; a plenary indulgence, along with communion (VIATICUM) all sin is forgiven; if granted (it usually is) (note: all sin IS forgiven, per James 5, 14-15) from GOD's word.

34.   My Skin Condition and Mass Healed (Sign of 9's)

(09 Apr 08) Wednesday: My skin condition (urticaria), I had for 18 years was healed (Note: I had asked the spirit for healing immediately after "the 2007 miracles of the Dome"; I am waiting for summer weather to verify this healing; so far it is valid as of 20 Jun 08 (Note: 21 Sept 08 healing is complete, skin is normal in the fall) this prayer was answered not only for the skin condition but also a mass (lump) on my upper right thigh disappeared.

35.   Blessed Virgin Mary's Sash Links With Sign of 9's, Delta no. 5

(03 Feb 08) Sunday: (see effect no. 31) Recall that this was concerning the blue sash with the statue match with the Dome (Note: Bible says, "GOD sits on a sapphire throne") (sign of 9's Delta no. 5 is effect no. 35 and this date 11 Feb 08 part of effect

no. 35 (remember this is the 150th anniversary of St. Bernadette of Lourdes).

36. Explanation For (NCIC) Cancels Website (Message no. 14) (Spirit Prompt)

(09 Mar 09) Monday: PROMPT FROM SPIRIT (NCIC) meaning, National Crime Information Center, is not equal to the web site according to the HOLY SPIRIT; it is equal to New Creature In Christ. (Note: Also sign of 9's on this date)

37. No. 7= "TOTALITY OF PERFECTION" (Seven Reconciliations In 2007) (message no. 15) (Spirit Prompt)

(07 Sept 09) Monday (Labor day): The no. 7 appeared on my upper right arm for 7 days after SPIRIT PROMPT to read miracle bible no. 611 completely; IT TOOK ME TWO YEARS. According to The Book of Revelation; there are seven spirits of GOD around the throne; put
in charge of the physical world; nations, communities (Churches) and individuals; these are the seven Angels or messengers of GOD; the no. 7 indicates TOTALITY OF PERFECTION. On this date I met a Chinese man named Tu Tran a friend and I was led back to our no. 611 Bible, now for sale at Nativity where I am; [Note: PROMPT FROM SPIRIT; I was told to reverse the nine on 9/11 (tragedy caused by Satan); it now becomes 611; the exact number of our (Fabian and I) miracle bible led to after my near-death experience; in addition, this shows that father Fullen was correct when he said, "Satan IS opposite JESUS" (911 vs. 611) (see effect no. 6) (Note: "9/11" New York towers disaster is now linked to my near-death experience.

38. Barbara's Healing Of Breast Cancer (Sign of 9's)

(09 Oct 09) (Note: Also Sign of 9's on this date) Monday: I met Mary's daughter Barbara who I had been praying for two years; since I met Mary (from Africa) at Nativity; she told me her daughter is completely healed of breast cancer (PRAISE GOD!) thanks Father; on that same day, I met a short women with black hair; one I had never seen at Nativity before; we walked into

church together and she asked, "how are you" I replied, "I'm great, especially since my near-death experience in 2007"; I told her about magnificence of the Dome of Creation, and she replied, "that's why we're here"; when we went through the doors of the church, I lost sight of her; I was unable to find her during mass and after mass, because Mary was introducing me to her daughter Barbara healed of breast cancer; who had a radical mastectomy and given only six months to live two years ago; an answer to our two year prayer, she becomes a "walking miracle" (Note: see effect no. 42) this one of the missed dates (Barbara's healing) miracles pearls or points on the straight line (09 Oct 07) falls on a Tuesday. AMEN!

39.   Discovery no. 2 of Miracle Bible no. 611 Since My Near-Death Experience (Message no. 17) (Spirit Prompt)

(17 Sept 09) Thursday (out of seq.): I checked with the secretary at Nativity; five no. 611 bibles came in on 06 Feb 09 (see effect no. 4) (bibles were purchased from "Renew Life La Salle") (whose life was renewed in 2007? MINE was); there are two bibles left on the shelf in the Nativity gift shop in the Vestibule of the church; PROMPT FROM SPIRIT in the middle of the night; I was told to translate this date back to 2007; when I did this, I found a sixth date, another point/pearl on my straight line function; re-calculating in my combination formula from math (see effect no. 30 page 16) I found the chances of this happening (using 6 in lieu of 5 dates) passing through my 70th birthday (see effect no. 30) to now increase from 5.3×10^{10} to 3.15×10^{12}; only GOD could do this; my further conclusion; this demonstrates GOD's awesome power (Note: this is exactly 2.8 years since my initial near-death experience).

40.   My Aunt Helen's Demise (Sign of 9's)

(09 Nov 09) (Note: Also Sign of 9's on this date) Monday: My aunt Helen's funeral and burial in Ohio; she was 93 years old (Rest In Glory) she passed on (05 Nov 09) I prayed her into heaven with the "JESUS crucified prayer."

41. Message no. 18 (Spirit Prompt) Math Explanation For 'Point In Space"

(22 Dec 09) Tuesday (Note: My birthday also falls on the 22nd of the month): I was awakened at 4:15 a.m. and received a message as PROMPT FROM SPIRIT; it said, "I was to recall what a (point in space) meant in math and apply that knowledge to the miracles; the point in this case or pearl is actually the leading edge of the continuous function (see effect no. 30 and 39(a straight line; perpendicular to the eye of the observer; this line would approach "infinity as a limit"; since by definition it IS a continuous function, meaning, other future significant supernatural events, dates, pearls, points or solutions are possible. Therefore the tile of my near-death experience now becomes "String of Pearls Miracles of the Dome of Creation" (see effect no. 1) further proof; a demonstration of the power of the HOLY SPIRIT.

42. Message no. 19 (Spirit Prompt) (no. 7 Meaning) Soul/Straight Line Analogy

(25 Dec 09) Friday (Christmas morning): I was awakened this time just before rising for the day (6:30 a.m.); I detected joy and knew that the spirit was giving me another message. It said, "the tan of my cover matches the (7)." It was trying to convey through my intellect, meaning, a power in the soul to recall the color of our no. 611 miracle bible, with the gold cross on the cover; immediately I knew the raised portion of the "7" that appeared on my arm and the cover, color, matched. I was also given in the same message by the spirit to translate the date (25th Christmas day) back to 2007; when I did this, going back to my miracle calendar (see graphics effect no. 30) the 25th of Dec 07 IS on a Tuesday; it now becomes a link to the Dome, my near-death experience; and it IS another pearl, point or solution to the straight line continuous function (see effect no. 39); this same message said, "pick up the missed dates"; in the process of looking at the calendar I did find two other missed dates (see effect no. 12) (pamphlet discovery and Barbara's cancer free) (see effect no. 38). I now have a total of nine solutions (Sign of 9's) to my straight line so far, miracle equation; using the combination formula again (nine dates in lieu six) and re-calculating the new combinations to now increase from 3.15

x10^{12} (occurrence probability) is rapidly going to zero where it always was) ASTRONOMICAL (2.9x10^{19}) meaning, 29 with 18 zeros after it, POSSIBLE COMBINATIONS using as before 365 days in 2007; indicating once again HOLY SPIRITS PRAYER POWER; from now on any future significant supernatural events will be translated back to 2007 to see if they fall on a Tuesday or Thursday; which would add more links, dates, pearls, events, leading back to the Dome experience and thus be considered miracles. These have been shown to be "The String Of Pearls Miracles Of the Dome of Creation." AMEN! I would like to digress at this point in the journal: the straight line is analogous to the immortal soul since both have a beginning but no end; in the straight line case the locus of points must remain on the straight line path, without deviation from that path; in addition, GOD is a being with NO BEGINNING, (HE is called the UNCAUSED CAUSE) from Philosophy of GOD (which I studied and selected as my non-technical elective at the university) it is how we can know some-things about HIM, through HIS effects (Note: see effect no. 12) meaning, knowing GOD through nature, by observing the effects in the world; but GOD can't ERROR because HE IS PERFECT; so HE NEVER DEVIATES from HIS Divine Will (Plan) for mankind analogous to the straight line AND FURTHER, GOD is EVERLASTING to EVERLASTING meaning, HE GOES ON FOREVER also similar to the straight line that's the REASON I KNOW GOD is using this straight line to PROVE THESE MIRACLES.

43.   Jim Rost And Lottery Similarity

(28 Dec 09) Monday: A technician (Jim Rost) that services garage doors; met him (21 Aug 09), told me HE had an out of body near-death experience similar to mine in the Iraq war. He was wounded in the "Battle of Fallujah" in 2007 and during his ordeal he was watching the battle take place BELOW HIM; he saw the enemy and his fellow infantry in a ferocious confrontation. His body was lying on the ground with two bullets in his back, but he was at peace. NO PAIN. When the battle confrontation concluded, he was rescued when he told me the actual date of his experience, I looked at my 2007 miracle calendar and noticed that BOTH dates

(21 Aug 09 translated to 2007 fall on a Tuesday) and (27 Sept 07) falls on a Thursday) are two more added solutions, pearls, points, to my straight line miracle equation; Jim now becomes linked to my near-death experience. A MAN I NEVER KNEW BEFORE; in addition, I found that this experience is identical to that of my 5th reconciliation with my brother William, before his passing on (see effect no. 25) and this date now becomes a single missed date; that increases the total number (from 9 to 12) this is what was meant when I concluded that future significant supernatural events, are possible, because this straight line or string of pearls is a function of TIME; substituting 12 for R in the combination formula where N=365 days/year; yields the following C=possible combinations=10^{24} (SUPER ASTRONOMICAL) calculating the occurrence probability=1 divided by C=0 as always indicating it is approaching zero as its limit, meaning, this is impossible; thus re-iterating ONLY GOD IS THE CAUSE. The following is a typical math calculation (Note: if one divides 10^{24} possible combinations by 7×10^{6}) meaning, 1 in 7 million estimated to win the lottery, the calculation yields 10^{18} (this number is called quintillion according to Webster Dictionary) meaning, I have won the lottery quintillion times; AMEN! (HOW ABOUT THAT FOR HOLY SPIRIT PRAYER POWER DEMONSTRATION?)

44.   Message no. 20 (Spirit Prompt) (no. 7 Significance)

(21 Jan 10) Thursday: PROMPT FROM SPIRIT at 2:15 a.m.; message, "I created the world in six days on the seventh day I rested"; my conclusion; this was a clear indication of additional significance of the no. 7 which appeared on my upper right arm after my complete reading of the entire no. 611 bible (see effect no. 37).

45.   Vehicle no. 1 Prayer Answered

(24 Mar 10) Wednesday: the day before this date (23 Mar 10) Tuesday; I also was in my 45th Novena (nine days of prayer Sign of 9's) asking the HOLY SPIRIT for a car to attend mass (since I had to turn-in my leased 2007 CTS Cadillac) the HOLY SPIRIT quickly answered on this date; I was led to the nearest GM dealer (Pallone Chevrolet) to a black 2009 (Sign of 9's again) Chevy

Impala 2LT Sedan, which I purchased in one-half day (another prayer answered) so the 24th of March now becomes the 19th point, pearl, or solution of my straight line miracle equation (translated back to 2007) because they are PARALLEL LINES; My conclusion: GOD is using translated, rather than transferred as HIS nomenclature, because it takes only two points/pearls to create a straight line continuous function; either before or beyond my 70th year experience; they are parallel equations [note: Since by definition the four equations (parallel lines) are in the same plane; they coincide with each other; they're collinear, through the process known as translation; thus adding one more link, date, pearl (19th) to the near-death experience] simply because it is ANOTHER PRAYER ANSWERED BY GOD (demonstrating once again the HOLY SPIRIT's prayer power) AMEN! It's superfluous, math speaking, to calculate possible combinations using 19 points; because the numbers are colossal; the probability of occurrence IS ZERO ALREADY; but I decided to go ahead and calculate 19 points in lieu of 12 points as previously mentioned effect no. 43 and the yield turns out to be 10^{32} using 19 points in the equations (that's decillion according to Websters Dictionary) an AWESOME NUMBER, that equals 1 with 32 zeros after it; this tells me to end the math right here; OUR HEAVENLY FATHER IS GREAT; but HE is using simple natural science (mathematics); to further validate, "The Straight Line/String of Pearls Miracles of the Dome of Creation."

46.   Message no. 21 (Spirit Prompt) (Proof of "Life After Life")

(30 Mar 10) Tuesday of HOLY WEEK: I received PROMPT FROM SPIRIT at 3 p.m. this afternoon; I was in the process of beginning my 46th Novena using my mom's large rosary (given to me by my brother Fabian) IT said, "use the journal FOR MY FATHER's GLORY! You have proof of LIFE AFTER LIFE; I WILL GUIDE YOU, DO NOT BE AFRAID." Note: this is the day I discovered missed dates, points, solutions to the straight line miracle equation; to now increase from (12 to 19 points/pearls); this is the MOST PROFOUND MESSAGE YET in a total of 38 months since my near-death experience.

47.   Message no. 22 (Spirit Prompt) (Gift "To The World")

(11 Apr 10) Sunday: I received PROMPT FROM SPIRIT at 8:30 a.m. on this "Divine Mercy Sunday"; the 2nd Sunday of Easter as follows, "give the journal as a gift from MY HOLY SPIRIT to the world, to demonstrate my spirits power and don't be concerned about Satan; I WILL NEUTRALIZE HIM; the gates of hell will not prevail against this"; (Note: on this date I recalled the song lyrics I composed for this miracle as follows: I did this immediately when I was sure that the HOLY SPIRIT IS THE CAUSE OF THIS GIFT; TITLE OF MY SONG; "They Didn't Believe Me" (an old favorite of Frank Sinatra, I just substituted MY lyrics) 1st verse; and when I told them how beautiful the Dome was, they didn't believe me, they didn't believe me 2nd verse: I tried and tried and tried again, till I was losing all my friends, but it was the most Heavenliest sight that one could see 3rd verse: And when I tell them and I'm certainly going to tell them that your HOLY SPIRIT came to HEAL and to FORGIVE ONLY ME, they'll NEVER believe me, they'll NEVER believe me, that from ALL YOUR CHILDREN OF GOD YOU'VE CHOSEN ME.

48.   Message no. 23 (Spirit Prompt) Near-Death Experience Dome Similar To St. Raymond

(14 Apr 10) Wednesday: I received a message at 1:36 a.m. on a PROMPT FROM SPIRIT as follows, "recall the Dome at St. Raymonds and you will understand my Dome; beware of jealous persons, I am with you." My discerning of this message is; that I DO remember the sanctuary Dome where the altar was; there was a hemispherical type blue Dome, but a deeper blue, than the creation Dome in my experience, in St. Raymonds case there was also a large cross of CHRIST crucified suspended from the ceiling at the apex by two chains. It was between the altar and the first pews; it was BEAUTIFUL; all this shows me that the explanation by Father Fullen IS AGAIN CORRECT; when he said, "it was her (Blessed Virgin Mary's) spouse, the HOLY SPIRIT, suspended from the apex of MY DOME"; thus in the architect's plan of St. Raymonds may have been an attempt to replicate the CREATION Dome; since my near-death experience occurred two weeks after joining St. Raymonds and the two Dome's are similar, except

no clouds (painted or otherwise) are depicted here; but we know that, JESUS=GOD=HOLY SPIRIT (three persons, one divine nature) meaning, where one IS, the other two have to be also; therefore, the HOLY SPIRIT must have been guiding me all along in IT'S plan to completely change my life, in an instant of time, that Jan 07 morning, by taking my soul to the Dome, and receiving the gifts of special graces, miracles, discernment and tongues; of course the bible says, "speaking in tongue" is lowest rung of the ladder; it is only for the people who don't know GOD, rather than for those who do know HIM and don't need signs of HIS infinite, mysterious power; of which tongues are nothing more than the spirit praying to the heavenly father; one cannot understand the language unless there is an interpreter around, which is very difficult, if not impossible to find thus the intended message is lost.

49.   Meeting no. 1 With Judy

(14 Apr 10) Wednesday: I met a woman named Judy at a Saturday Vigil mass (03 mar 10) who wanted to sit in my pew, because she said, "she enjoyed my singing" I said, "I didn't own the pew" and she sat on the end adjacent to the center aisle; I noticed she was on crutches and that she began to sob unceasingly; I asked, "why are you crying?" she said, "she just lost her 44 year old brain diseased son and was heartbroken" the same reason she lost use of her legs, that same day; while we continued to get acquainted, she said, "she HAD ALSO had a near-death experience"; we then compared each others notes; she went through a tunnel and peered over the edge at its ends and saw a magnificent blue sky with a white light approaching her; then she felt being drawn back down the tunnel and to her body, during a heart meditation procedure; her son Patrick had passed on (07 Feb 10) recall the 7 meaning in my experience, "TOTALITY OF PERFECTION"; one thing led to another and she wanted a a partial first draft of my journal to which I complied, she ended up purchasing the last no. 611 bible with a tan cover at Nativity gift shop; we had both the journal and the no. 611 bible blessed by Father Wilson; the next week, she was a COMPLETELY CHANGED PERSON; she had read my journal over and over again in conjunction with her no. 611 bible

and she told me they BOTH seemed to have INSPIRATIONAL HEALING POWER (the HOLY SPIRIT works in mysterious ways). AMEN! We are now very good friends, additionally, I prevented her from wanting to be with her son Patrick, who is now in heaven receiving his reward from GOD; I gave her the JESUS crucified prayer to assure his arrival in heaven; everyday she tells me now that she reads my journal and finds something new; SHE HAS GAINED MUCH STRENGTH.

50. Pamela (DMV Meeting) Ken And Jennifer

(15 Apr 10) Thursday: I met a woman in the Department of Motor Vehicles (DMV) in the mall; it was odd how we met; there were maybe 30 empty seats and she sat down next to me; now seats are tied to one another and she could have sat anywhere; she was a younger woman, Hispanic in nature; I'm not sure; we said hello and we introduced ourselves; she said "her name was Pamela"; I assumed she was there to renew her driver's license; we didn't discuss that; instead I turned the conversation to my near-death experience because I was being motivated by the spirit to comply with the spirits wishes; I was feeling at the time; her eyes immediately widened; she looked astonished ; a big smile came over her face and she asked what happened to me in 2007; after I described the "Dome of Creation" she was flabbergasted and wanted me to continue my 2007 experiences; we were interrupted because our numbers were called to conduct our business at our respective awaiting DMV personal window; when our business concluded we met again and walked out together; we were standing in the mall about 30 feet outside (Target) the nearest store; I told her about being led to the no. 611 miracle bible, the HOLY SPIRIT pamphlet and the two shots of the overwhelming, identical joy, after the Dome near-death experience; I gave her my cell phone number and told her I was now at Nativity she accepted both and said "she was very interested to hear more and she knew where the church of Nativity was in Burke" (she had also mentioned earlier "give the journal to the world" same as spirits prompt) she also said as she past in front of me heading for Target on my left "she would contact me." I watched her as she approached the entrance as I was moving towards the mall exit which was about

30 feet straight ahead; I happened to turn to look back to my left and she was GONE. I had a clear view of the entrance and there were NO people in the vicinity; estimating her velocity of her approach at about 30 feet/5 seconds; she couldn't have walked fast and disappear in 5 seconds; my conclusion; if I don't hear from her within a week or so, I must conclude she was an ANGEL; because she becomes the fourth person to disappear since the final mass I attended at St. Raymond; update: I decided to contact "Target store in mall" (18 Apr 10) Sunday to see if a woman named "Pamela" was an employee; the answer was negative; (an Angel? Your conclusion) there was Ken Steiner (who told me about his vision and conversion, reconciliation with his wife, that very evening after he arrived home from work); it happened in his car while he was stopped at a red light I never saw him again either, although he said, "he attended 6:30 a.m. mass everyday and parked next to me everyday; I called St. Raymond rectory and the woman told me there wasn't any Ken Steiner registered just another event in my life after the Dome (see effect no. 22) about Jennifer whom I met at St. Bernadettes; a church I was a member of for 23 years before the spirit led me to Nativity; she had told me about her similar near-death experience; where she had a heart attack while her daughter an EMT, was home for lunch; she said while her daughter was performing CPR on her; she was out of her body sitting in an adjacent chair watching her; she was revived and recovered; Jennifer said, "she was going home to give her children their lunch but would call me immediately after"; so we could compare notes; I never heard from her or saw her again and no one I talked to had either; just another mystery in this continuing adventure (see effect no. 38) for the 4th person in my experience I couldn't find; the same morning I was introduced to Mary's daughter Barbara completely healed of cancer (a very significant prayer answered) she is truly " A WALKING MIRACLE"; I want to emphasize this to you, reader; Barbara is a special child of GOD and he has rewarded her, by giving her at age 45 a new life for HIS purpose; similar to when I was given the same in 2007. Barbara and I because of our unique experiences now become linked to one another, to deliver GOD's message to YOUR world; by these supernatural events, he demonstrates always HIS infinite love (it's

called, AGAPE, perfect love) despite our transgressions against HIM.

51. My Dad's Wrist-Watch Link With My Near Death-Experience And Donna's NDE---

(01 May 10) Saturday: I decided on this date to overhaul my dad's wrist watch given to me a as remembrance of his passing (11 May 72), 38 years later, to open the ring case I had left it in for safe keeping when I opened the case the 2nd hand was running; the WATCH WAS RUNNING; I was astonished and so was the jeweler I gave it to for the overhaul; he said, "it shouldn't have been working since it was too old, to have a self-winding, or kinetic movement, capability"; its your decision reader; natural cause or supernatural cause? After contemplating my decision, I added this event as my 23rd number of points/ pearls or solutions to the miracle equation (Y1=70) (see effect no. 30) of course by translating this date to 2007; it falls on a Tuesday, exactly on the main equation; calculating the possible combinations for 23 points yields 10^{36}; this is called "undecillion" in Webster Dictionary; the probability of occurrence is still zero. Once again GOD's HOLY SPIRIT flexing HIS muscle; my conclusion; additionally, on this day I met Donna; who I didn't knew at the time was a non-Catholic; yet she sat right down next to me at the first communion mass; she was there, I found later in our acquaintance and conversation; because her friends daughter received her first communion; Donna was there with her daughter Michelle; she introduced me to her daughter and I told them about my near-death experience and Donna especially was more interested had also a near-death encounter with GOD; so after mass we compared notes; she said, "during my operation I was aware of my soul leaving my body and being in the presence of a beautiful white light and she was also aware of a hand on her shoulder behind her, when she turned to see who it was, she couldn't see HIS face, because light was so bright, but she knew it was God's HOLY SPIRIT"; what happened next, I found hard to believe at first; but realizing the power GOD possesses I knew she was truthful; she told me the spirit gave her a glimpse of her body reuniting with her soul and in an instant she was back in the operating room recovering from her ordeal and from the look on

her face, it wasn't a dream. I had told her about my intentions to complete my journal and she

immediately asked me if I could get her a copy because she soon would be leaving the country; I detected the urgency in her voice and complied; taking a partial first draft copy to the dentist office where her daughter Michelle worked; I never received any feedback from her, but I had received discernment from my dome experience and I knew she would receive the help and the answers she was looking for; it was automatic for me; it suffices to say that Donna's experience further demonstrates God's mysterious ways of opening our eyes; the main reason for this journal. I obviously don't consider these last two events miracles, Donna's was; but certainly my dad's watch running after 38 years isn't one, because our creator is always interested in the BIG picture; how do these events relate to our salvation? How does it change our personal relationship with GOD our HEAVENLY FATHER?

52.   Martine, Nina And Judy Link With My Near- Death Experience

(03 May 10) Monday: This morning I was led by the spirit to Martine (see effect no. 53 and 161) once "special Angel" and led to another one in the afternoon. I was visiting the mall as I had done many times while living in Virginia; it was a typical hot summer day and I went to Spencer's gift store just looking, not buying, as I exited the store, the spirit turned to me to the right, and there she was selling cell phones in a booth for AT&T. I approached her and commented on the emptiness of the mall due to the bad economy; I noticed how beautiful she was; of course, I'm a typical male and she agreed with me on the condition of the mall and she also was a frequent visitor; her name was Saturnina but she preferred to be known as Nina. I introduced myself and asked, "if she believed in miracles"; by the way that opening was given to me by the HOLY SPIRITS PROMPT one night. Nina said, "she did", and I found out she was a Filipino; also catholic; I related my experience to her and she wanted to know more; making a long story short, she accepted a copy of my first draft journal and of the miracle no. 611 bible (05 May 10) with the most beautiful smile I had ever seen. Nina, Martine and Judy are considered pearls, precious gems on the string of pearls of the Dome; Everytime I

visit her in the mall to keep her company, because she has very few customers, she exhibits that smile; this is GODS HOLY SPIRIT in action, gathering more people for HIS elect. In reality I consider my meeting Nina, Martine and Judy as three of the best events of my life; the first of course will always be my encounter with the "Dome Of Creation" on the morning of (09 Jan 07). I didn't realize it at the time but deciding to examine the date (03 May 10) falling on a Thursday; that day of our first meeting; Nina and Martine now become linked to my near- death experience translating back to 2007 and thus the 24th and 25th point, pearl, or solution to the main miracle equation Y1=70; but additional need for math calculation is unnecessary because I have sufficient data for my conclusion as to these post- evidentiary events and definitely suggestive of supernatural cause. Additionally, I met Judy on the (03 March 10) in much the same way; the HOLY SPIRIT selects and leads me and has been leading me from the return of my soul to my body on that beautiful day in January 2007; reiterating the best day in my entire life; (at this point in my life) so for this reason Judy lies in what I call "The Plane Of The Pearls" and she becomes the 22nd pearl, point or solution to my miracle equation (see effect no. 30) because I consider these events mentioned above as significant; they are just not random dates as far as GOD is concerned; because he is the only perfect being in existence and planned my path to Nina, Martine and Judy before he created and RE-CREATED ME; what an AWESOME, wonderful and loving CREATOR we have, what HE'S done for me, as the song goes, he will do for you.

53.   Meeting no. 1 With Martine Link With My Near-Death Experience

(20 May 10) Thursday: This Thursday I was delivering a brand new upgraded no. 611 miracle bible, green hard cover version, to a woman named Martine; whom I had met in this manner; she came and sat down in my pew (03 May 10) Monday much the same way as Judy did, the handicap woman who had just lost her 44 year old son Patrick (see effect no. 49)I introduced myself to Martine and we began our acquaintance; I asked her, "do you believe in miracles" her answer was, "yes I do"; then I told her about my near- death experience; she was listening intently and

wanted to hear more about it and we continued the conversation after mass, outside the church; she told me, "she was from Africa and new to the area"; when I related my experience to her she immediately wanted to have the bible with the Dome in it; which was of course the miracle bible no.611; she gave me the money for it and I went to Jermantown Center in Fairfax to purchase the bible; I also gave her a copy of a partial first draft of the journal, which would give her a synopsis of my journey so far; she went away happy; as I know the HOLY SPIRIT will give her total joy as HE did me.

54.   My 73rd Birthday Link With Pentecost

(22 May 10) Saturday: My 73rd birthday coincided with the "Vigil of Pentecost" this year; the bible says, "we walk by faith and not by sight", but my encounter with the Dome proves I received and continue to receive both. I have replaced the term "belief" with "know" in the investigation of these events; reiterating from my preface of this journal.

55.   Satan's Second Attack

(21 Jun 10) Monday: On this date I experienced fear at 3:52 a.m. this morning, when I received a prompt just before the end of what Father Fullen had said, "was considered the devils hour" (see effect no. 6) I knew this couldn't have been from the HOLY SPIRIT because it was still within the hour; this was Satan's attempt to derail the writing of this journal; the prompt told me, "GO DOWNSTAIRS AND THROW EVERYTHING AWAY. NOTHING IS WORKING." I almost complied with this request; for I was experiencing some discouragement of late knowing I had a lot of work remaining to complete this journal, so I started praying as Father Fullen had suggested and I knew Satan was again neutralized because the journal had been blessed and as the spirit is protecting it, I must continue and ignore Satan's attacks.

56.   First Shift Of Journal Focus

(01Oct 07) Monday (out of seq.): I would like to now shift my focus of the journal from the mathematics (the numbers) and equations connected to this experience, exclusively to petitions asked and answered, by the HOLY SPIRIT, the center of the "Dome Of Creation" and to the individuals I encountered on this journey through time and criminals which I know were brought to justice so far; as well as other petitions or prayers answered due to the HOLY SPIRITS WILL: some of them may be redundant; but all are necessary as a revelation of GOD HIMSELF, to all who read this journal; flashing back to those previous years at Nativity as mentioned below.

57.   Clara And Elizabeth

(02 Oct 07) (out of seq.) Tuesday 7:30 am. mass I met a beautiful Korean lady, tall and statuesque, named Clara; she was sitting and always sits in the first pew able to accommodate three people. I was led by the HOLY SPIRIT to the second pew directly behind her but to her left. I have been sitting in the same place for almost 3 years now. Another older lady, Elizabeth also a Korean, unable to care for herself and always exiting from a walker utilized by her caretaker everyday; sitting with Clara. I introduced myself as I was led by the spirit to do so and related my near-death experience; they both wanted me to give them the detailed account as they were astonished; both believing in miracles and specifically in mine; telling me to add their request to my prayer list and they would reciprocate. Clara requested her business would be sold so she could concentrate on taking care of her family, while her husband, a lobbyist, would continue to be successful to fulfill his obligations to the family consisting of two children, Lydia and Joseph. My first prayer request was answered (14 Jul 08) and I knew my so called "HOT LINE TO THE HOLY SPIRIT" was established; this was the beginning of a successful long prayer list over-time, encouraging me and introducing another avenue for proof of, "The String Of Pearls Miracles Of The Dome Of Creation". AMEN! Additionally, Elizabeth would have a big problem necessitating HOLY SPIRIT intervention when she left mass in March 2010 due to a fall and a serious hip injury. When I discovered why

she wasn't attending mass (as she usually went to daily mass as I did) after my post near-death prompt, for me to attend mass everyday and GOD blessed me with our meeting each other. I prayed earnestly for her healing and return to mass. This prayer was answered and she returned on (07 Apr 10) approximately one month later; if that doesn't convince my readers of GODS healing power, nothing will; because she is now 90 years old and still sitting in the same pew with me directly behind her and watching over her everyday; she loves me and I love her as GODS child and she is very happy that I hold her hands while looking into those beautiful eyes everyday; almost 3 years since we first met, she is a widow and her husband passed on before the HOLY SPIRIT led me to Nativity and to her that Tuesday in October 2007.

58.   Joined Nativity Parish

(11 Oct 07) Thursday: Today I became an official parishioner of Nativity church by registering my name with the parish. According to my miracle calendar this would have been my 26th point, pearl or solution to my miracle equation. I don't need additional points or math calculation, but this is only more icing on the cake.

59.   Meeting no. 2 With Father Daniel

(16 Oct 07) Tuesday: I met Father Daniel from Kenya, Africa, visiting Nativity for four weeks. I told him about my encounter with the Dome and he immediately wanted to see my post-evidentiary effects; he believed I did receive the HOLY SPIRITS special graces; the same conclusion as Father Jack Fullen (rest in glory); I was being touched by GOD with miracles and I was selected to deliver the message to all of GODS people. He asked me to PRAY FOR HIM after he blessed me (see effect no. 27).

60.   Barbara Is My "Walking Miracle"

(23 Nov 07) Friday: I met Mary (visiting her daughter from Africa) and we immediately connected because of her knowledge of my near-death experience. She wanted me to add Barbara to my prayer list to which I complied and she said, "her daughter had a radical mastectomy due to breast cancer and was given six months to live".

I added her to my Novena's (9 days of prayer) and kept her there. After two years of prayer Mary finally introduced me (see effect no. 38 and 50) to her on (09 Oct 09) Sign Of 9's, completely cleared and healed of cancer. We all REJOICED that wonderful day, a further demonstration of the HOLY SPIRITS awesome healing power; another miracle attributable to MY Dome. She is definitely a "WALKING MIRCLE"; and now becomes a precious gem, a pearl and the 8th miracle of the Dome and would have been the 27th point; translated back to 2007 from October 2009, our first meeting date.

61.   Father Wilson (HE BELIEVES)

(24 Nov 07) Saturday: I introduced myself to Father Wilson of Nativity and related my encounter with the Dome. He also believed and asked ME TO PRAY FOR HIM; I noticed, like so many other men called by GOD to the priesthood, he was also having doubts of his vocation (apparently since they are human beings) Satan attacks them when they are vulnerable.

62.   Research Of "HOLY SPIRIT Pamphlet"

(29 Nov 07) Thursday: In the process of researching the origin of the "HOLY SPIRIT PAMPHLET", my third miracle; I phoned a woman named Madalyn Baer, who worked for St. Anthony Messenger Press, in Cincinnati Ohio (see effect no. 12) after telling her why I needed information about the pamphlet, she was also astonished when I explained my Dome experience and asked me to put her family on my prayer list; I did. She also requested a copy of my journal at that point and accepted my MOM'S prayer; which she believed all the evidence I sent her and framed the prayer and kept it on her desk, for all her colleagues to observe; on (04 Dec 07) she said my prayer was answered her family is fine and the following words are quotes from the letter she sent me; "thank you for sharing your amazing experience with me. Your journal with the prayer from your mother was received and I will pray it and pass it on to others"; simply another demonstration of GODS healing power; THE DOME STRIKES AGAIN; she could have been the 28th point, pearl or solution to the straight line miracle equation (Y1=70) if I needed additional proof; WHICH I DON'T.

Remember reader I hadn't discovered my miracle calendar linear relationship with all events in 2007 until (25 Jan 08) (see graphics effect no. 30).

63.   Meeting no. 1 With Ginger And Bishop Zubik

(29 Dec 07) Saturday: I was led by the HOLY SPIRIT to Ginger she was 65 years old a little younger than me, in the front pew next to me. I related my experience as usual to comply with HOLY SPIRITS request to "DELIVER THE MESSAGE TO MY PEOPLE". She was also vulnerable to miracles, a widow and very interested in my experience. Immediately I noticed a cast on her left wrist and she said she broke her wrist and was told it would take 6-8 weeks to heal. Upon hearing this I asked her if she would allow me to add her to my Novena prayer list (90 percent of my prayers had been answered to date) and I knew she needed intervention; bottom line is, she was healed completely and absolutely in only 4 WEEKS TIME; another success for my heavenly father; WE BOTH REJOICED; after mass I met Bishop David Zubik from Pittsburgh Pennsylvania; who had said the mass. In the vestibule of the church he greeted us as we were leaving; to make a long story short, I related my experiences of the Dome and its aftermath and he said, "speak out to all who will listen; they didn't believe JESUS when HE was on this earth either"; also said, "I was being touched by GOD, our creator, in a very special way"; each time we meet now he gives me the same response. That very day of helping Ginger and meeting David, a crisis developed when I returned home that very morning; an ambulance was called to my neighbor's house, Jackie next door; I raced over to help, but they were transporting her to the emergency room; I immediately sprung into prayer action to the HOLY SPIRIT; asking HIM to intervene. Jackie was 60 years old at the time and I had previously told her about my Dome experience; she also believed in the miracles; I wasn't worried because GOD had shown me HIS healing power throughout 2007; the next day I noticed her out by her mailbox and I went over to see how big the problem may have been; she answered the door with a sad look on her face; I proceeded to inquire about her sadness; she said, "she had to take some tests tomorrow"; I laid my right hand on her

shoulder and said, "the HOLY SPIRIT will be with you; don't be afraid"; well, GODS healing power comes to the fore again; ALL TESTS WERE NEGATIVE; the following day she related that to me, by her mailbox and I noticed the smile on that beautiful face of hers. AMEN! By the way, Jackie has been taken care of her son Michael, since he was injured in an auto accident and is confined to a wheelchair.

64.   Amber (Saleswoman)

(01 May 08) Thursday: A saleswoman named Amber called on me; upon answering the door she said, "she was collecting funds for handicap children" and showed me her credentials, to which I complied; she told me, "she believed in miracles" and wanted to help; after I told her of the journey the HOLY SPIRIT wanted me to travel to deliver HIS message; I had in my possession 51 copies of my MOM'S prayer; she read it and loved it; took one for herself and volunteered to deliver the remaining 50 to the neighbors in my development; she took my cell phone number and would call me to inform me of their acceptance/rejection that day; just to show the HOLY SPIRITS power once again. She made an affirmative call to me that evening, comparing this date with respect to my miracle calendar; I found that the translation process 2008 to 2007; would have been the 28th point, pearl or solution to (Y1=70) she had successfully delivered ALL FIFTY PRAYERS.

65.   Jim Rost Links With 3 Pearls

(21 Aug 09) Friday: Chronologically speaking this date is VERY IMPORTANT because I first met Jim Rost, my garage door technician, whose near-death experience in Iraq LINKED TO MINE (see effect no. 30 and 43 for details) a man that I was destined by GOD to meet; to which I gave a copy of MOMS prayer and later thanked the HOLY SPIRIT for this special persons entrance into my life; (3 points, pearls or solutions are associated with our destiny).

66.   Rick (Holy spirit Prayer Answered)

(07 Sept 09) Monday Labor Day: I met Rick, "A Knight Of Columbus" member and he verified the significance and importance of the no. 7 in my no. 611 miracle bible; after I related my experiences with him; he received a copy of my first draft of the journal knowing that it may possess, as it has for Judy and others, healing and inspirational power in dealing with problems he was having in his family; I found out later that the HOLY SPIRIT did correct the situation; another prayer answered.

67.   Keith (Holy spirit Prayer Answered)

(11 Sept 09) Friday 8th anniversary of the tragedy caused by Satan in New York city: I met Keith an African-American at my grocery store; he was astonished and interested, as all others were of my near-death experience and wanted me to add his problem to my prayer list; 2 weeks later he informed me that my intervention had solved the problem at home; another prayer answered, additionally, all future links to 9/11 (see effect no. 37) are automatically connected to the no. 611 miracle bible and thus to my Dome experience; always demonstrating HOLY SPIRIT PRAYER POWER.

68.   Meeting no. 2 With Ginger

(23 Oct 09) Tuesday: This date would have become my 29th point, pearl or solution to my miracle equation (Yl=70) translated back to 2007 from 2009; because it falls on a Tuesday also in 2007 here's how it transpired involving Ginger again (see effect no. 63) the last time I saw Ginger she was on crutches and I asked her what happened, she said, "while looking after her grandchildren, since she was now a grandma; she fell hard on her left knee and it was in a cast to facilitate the healing" but she also said, the prognosis was, "she may never walk again without crutches and could spend the rest of her life confined to a wheelchair"; immediately I put her at the top of my novena prayer list; approximately 6 weeks before; asking the HOLY SPIRIT to again intervene; for the 2nd time involving one wonderful soul; my friend Ginger; never before had I ever requested a double- healing; WELL, LOW AND BEHOLD ON THIS DATE IT HAPPENED; a double-healing for Ginger;

"A double-whammy, if you will"; she is walking again as she did before her accident and we DOUBLED OUR REJOICING TO THE HOLY SPIRIT; I am not labeling this a miracle; because I don't know if she had the correct evaluation; she never obtained a second prognosis; Ginger, a widow is fine now and has moved to Missouri to begin a new life watching over those same grandchildren full time while both parents are working.

69.   Janet (Led By Spirit)

(08 May 10) Saturday: I didn't know that at this date that our beloved Father Jack Fullen had passed on (see effect no. lB) the day before; I was looking for his sick bay where I was told he was, when the HOLY SPIRIT led me to a woman in the parking area of the hospice, off route 29 in Fairfax; her name was Janet and using her GPS on her cell phone she told me I was in the correct development and we started getting acquainted, so I took this opportunity (as the spirit led me) to inform her of my encounter with the "Dome Of Creation"; of course; as all are usually interested in my near-death experience, she wanted me to reveal the details; after providing the necessary information, she believed in my miracle and said, "although I'm not catholic", of which I commented, "it doesn't matter because this is from GOD to all people here and around the world; the main purpose of my journal"; she said, "she would purchase a copy of the no. 611 miracle bible; because of not only my experience, but her children wanted her to read the bible and had been encouraging her to do so." I also provided a copy of my journal and she wanted to read it to her children; she said, "indeed you are a messenger and GOD is going to reward you"; HE ALREADY HAS; Janet said, "she and her children will pray for the journal's success"; she gave me her phone number to keep in touch; I decided to examine this meeting date and discovered this would have been my 30th point, pearl or solution to (Y1=70) because it fell exactly on the straight line function; translated back to 2007; falling on a Tuesday; compliments of GODS HOLY SPIRIT POWER.

70.   Darthula (Healed Through Prayer)

(05 Jun 10) Saturday: I was attending 5 p.m. Vigil mass as I'm accustomed to, sitting with my friends Mike and Mary; when a woman sat next to me at the end of the pew and smiled at me; we were singing, "the entrance of the mass song" and she joined in also; at the songs conclusion I informed her that I loved to sing and she replied, "she did too and that she just heard an Angel in my singing"; I said, "your putting me on"; that was the beginning of our acquaintance; her name was Darthula; it was the spirit again taking the initiative with our meeting; for I took the opportunity, as always the spirit led me, to tell her about my experience with the Dome. We continued our conversation in the vestibule after mass and she informed me of her healing, through prayer of her, "rheumatoid arthritis" and understood the meaning of TRUE miracles; which she agreed mine was; WE BOTH REJOICED; the spirit brought us together, that night and she also wanted a copy of my journal. I mailed her one along with the journals companion the no. 611 miracle bible; she later thanked me with all her heart. I again decided to examine this date with respect to my 2007 miracle calendar (see graphics effect no. 30) and found this would have been my 31st point, pearl or solution to my now familiar miracle equation (Yl=70) translated back to 2007; this date falls on a Tuesday also; HOLY SPIRITS POWER STRIKES AGAIN.

71.   Angelic And meeting no. 2 With Martine And Salman

(26 Jun 10) Saturday: After attending my customary morning 9 a.m. mass I met two women in succession one named Angelic (with a baby in a stroller) and Martine for the second time in the car next to me in the parking lot; the spirit led me to them as usual. Angelic after our acquaintance wanted me to show her the no. 611 bible with the Dome; I entered the gift shop in the vestibule of the church and found 7 new green hard cover bibles; having been delivered, upon my inquiry, the day before, according to the clerk; I took one without paying, saying, "I just want to show it to Angelic"; the clerk said, "okay" but followed me to her; I showed her the Dome on page 5 of Genesis and she decided to purchase it, because she also believed in. "The String Of Pearls Miracles

Of The Dome Of Creation"; but I informed her, "I didn't have a copy of the journal to give her but that she could read it upon its release to the public"; she accepted my explanation and said, "we were brought together by the spirit." I left Angelic and her baby and was returning to my car in the parking lot; I was led again by the spirit to Martine (see effect no. 53) next to my vehicle, who looked a little sad; she said, "she was new to the area from Africa and it was difficult for her and her 17 year old daughter Anne to begin her new life as a nanny." I took the opportunity again, as the spirit leads me to make her acquaintance informing her of my experiences in these past 42 months; after the very best day of my life (09 Jan 07); immediately she was astonished and gave me a beautiful smile and showed her appreciation of my intervention; by asking me for a copy of my journal; I said, "I will bring you one next Saturday if you are attending this same mass"; she said, "she would meet me after mass"; to which I replied, "don't forget also the Dome bible no. 611, its companion"; the next week she received both and thanked me for our meeting each other; saying, "I was truly what she needed" to begin her new life for the LORD; she's well-adjusted now and tells me she's very happy; my reader; that is again HOLY SPIRIT power; that same evening I met Salman, who works with Nina at the mall, where I would sing to Nina, so as to alleviate her boredom, since she has few customers and to my surprise it turned out that he was a computer science graduate from India; looking for a job and willing to relocate; I told him I would help him. I called some contacts for him; but I couldn't reach them; he was also proficient in math and I asked him to check my math calculations regarding the miracle and he said, "THEY WERE CORRECT"; this happened to be the very first time on this journey, that the spirit led me to three different individuals; Angelic, Martine and a young man Salman; who agreed with my conclusions of the Dome in the same day; it should be noted that Salman was here working for only two months; the main reason for not having employment in his field of computers. He needed to be here as an American citizen with at least five months residency; this indicates HOLY SPIRIT power is non-discriminating.

72. Ann (3rd Anniversary of HOLY SPIRIT Pamphlet Discovery)

(28 Jun 10) Monday: A significant date today, marking the third anniversary of my being led by the HOLY SPIRIT to the 1995 pamphlet in 2007, my third miracle (see effect no. 12 and 30 on my miracle graphics); this time I was led to a woman named Ann; with the same type and color, year vehicle as mine; we always were confused about this; in fact that's how our acquaintance began; I disclosed the miracle and she was astonished and believed and said, "you have power"; I replied, "only prayer power given to me from the Dome by the HOLY SPIRIT"; upon investigating this date I discovered this would have been double or two concentric circles around '28 on my miracle calendar"; translated back to 2007, of course and would also have been my 32nd point, pearl or solution to (Y1=70) a mere formality for HOLY SPIRIT "DOUBLE-WHAMMY POWER".

73. Joeyao (Only Chinese Man Linked With My Near-Death Experience And Blessed Virgin Mary)

(30 Jun 10) Wednesday: On this date I ran into a Chinese man named Joeyao; in a supermarket and literally we did bump into each other, physically and apologized to one another; he was very nice and to my surprise an engineer like me, fancy that! One thing led to another and our conversation turned to my Dome experience; to my astonishment he said, "he believed in the HOLY SPIRIT, the VIRGIN MARY and the existence of GOD"; he wanted to see my journal which I happened to have in my vehicle; to which I complied; we went to the parking lot and I let him read what I had brought with me; it wasn't complete, but enough that he said, "you are a modern day prophet I corrected him and said, "only a messenger endowed by the HOLY SPIRIT"; he also said, "he needed to be closer to GOD and thanked me for my intervention in his life"; I told him, "I will pray for you and your family".

74. Family no. 1 Healed (involving Dog Casey)

(24 Jun 10) (out of seq.) Thursday: I'm only mentioning this date because it's unusual; involving a healing of my brothers beloved dog Casey, a black Labrador retriever, whom he requested my

novena prayer intervention on two occasions (07 Jul 08 and approximately 10 Jun 10) and the HOLY SPIRIT came to the fore again; completely healing Casey's serious illness twice; another "DOUBLE-WHAMMY" by GODS power; two home runs in the vernacular of baseball; one of my favorite sports; earlier other healing's of HOLY SPIRIT prayer intervention happened in the same family; my niece Robin on one occasion (03 Sept 08) an inner ear problem healed and my brother Fabian healed on three occasions; once for healing of his left ankle, after successful (06 Aug 09) surgery; injured in a motorcycle accident and (09 Mar 10) heart test and finally an absolute and complete healing of a torn cartilage in his left knee also through surgery is depending on HOLY SPIRIT PRAYER POWER! Now will answer once more; but in these cases in an entire family; my brother being 78 years old at the time.

75. Christina Applegate Link With My Near-Death Experience And Blessed Virgin Mary

(15 Aug 08) (Out of seq.) Friday: This date was, "The Assumption Of The Blessed Virgin Mary" and a very loved person an actress Christina Applegate was completely healed of breast cancer and successful breast reconstruction; after my novena prayers for her were answered again.

76. Journalist Saberi Released

(11 May 09) (Out of seq.) Monday: Another novena prayer of mine was answered when a female journalist was released, unharmed, from an Iranian jail where she was being held; her name was Saberi and her family was very happy, especially her sister, who had been working tirelessly for her successful return home. HOLY SPIRIT intervention, another similar event happened (05 Aug 09) this time involving two journalists successfully released unharmed from a North Korean prison; again due to HOLY SPIRIT direct intervention, as I prayed earnestly for this wonderful outcome.

77. Second Shift Of Journal (CPA And WPA Meaning)

(29 Jan 08) (out of seq.) Tuesday: I would again like to shift my focus of this journal to my favorite mission for the HOLY SPIRIT; BRINGING ALL TYPES OF CRIMINALS TO JUSTICE, both civilian and military or war prayers answered; meaning, (CPA) for civilian prayers answered including non-criminal types and (WPA) for war prayers. I will, in most cases, simply list them, and their result; I am a sleuth for GOD, since HE returned me to the world, for HIS purpose NOT mine; another part of my mission on earth.

78. Brianna Denison (Rest In Glory) RIG (CPA no. 1)

(26 Nov 08) (out of seq.) Wednesday: Biela finally captured and charged with first degree murder, rape and kidnapping (17 Feb 09) of a beautiful coed, Brianna Denison (RIG), meaning, "REST IN GLORY"; she finally received justice after almost three months. (CPA) Thanks FATHER!

79. Florida Rapist caught Immediately (CPA no. 2)

(13 Apr 08) (out of seq.) Sunday: Rapist using an ATM of a female victim in Florida, caught on video the VERY NEXT DAY, after my prayer intervention. (CPA) Thanks Heavenly Father!

80. Nancy Cooper (Rest In Glory) RIG (CPA no. 3)

(28 Oct 08) (out of seq.) Tuesday: Nancy Cooper's husband arrested for her first degree murder while jogging; almost three months after her body was found RIG Nancy! (CPA) Thanks LORD!

81. Marine Nurse (Rest In Glory) RIG (CPA no. 4)

(14 Jul 08) (out of seq.) Monday: A marine was charged with first degree murder of his wife, also a marine, after one week; marine nurse RIG. (CPA) Thanks LORD!

82. Caylee Anthony (Rest In Glory) RIG (CPA no. 5)

(19 Jul 08) (out of seq.) Saturday: Caylee Anthony RIG, 2 years old and would have been 3 years had she reached (09 Aug 08) my 1st anniversary of my 4th miracle (see effect no. 18); her body was discovered (11 Dec 08) in a swamp near her Florida home; her mother Casey Anthony, was arrested and is in jail, in Florida until her trial scheduled for May 2011. Caylee didn't receive justice. (05 Jul 11) Tuesday: She was found "not guilty" by the jury, but I know this was a miscarriage of justice and I am praying earnestly for God to judge her to hell for all eternity because his word says "no murderer will ever enter the Kingdom of Heaven." Remember God is unchangeable so she is already destined for Hell.

83. O.J. Simpson Arrested (CPA no. 6)

(03 Oct 08) (out of seq.) Friday: My nemesis, O.J. Simpson finally arrested and sentenced to 33 years in prison for armed robbery and assault; Ron Goldman and Nichole Simpson finally getting justice for their brutal slaying on the very same day in '95' of his arrest; he was sentenced on (05 Dec 08); a big thanks to my HEAVENLY FATHER and an answer to millions of prayers including mine since '95'. (CPA)

84. Pressly (Rest In Glory) RIG (CPA no. 7)

(27 Nov 08) Thanksgiving Day Thursday (Out of seq.): Curtis Vance arrested and given life without parole, for the brutal slaying of a beautiful and popular anchor woman named Pressly RIG. (CPA) Thank you FATHER!

85. Balfour Arrested (CPA no. 8)

(02 Dec 08) (out of seq.) Tuesday: Balfour arrested and charged with the murder of three of Jennifer Hudson's family and given the death sentence. (CPA) Thanks again FATHER!

86. Mumbai Attacks Arrested 20 Militants (WPA no. 1)

(09 Dec 08) (out of seq.) Tuesday: On the (Sign Of 9's) twenty arrested for the Mumbai attacks in India; (179 dead, 200 wounded)

on (28 Nov 08); perpetrated by a group called, "LET" out of Pakistan; (WPA) Thanks LORD! Also MELE was arrested on this same day and given his death sentenced for brutal murder of Laura Garza (19 years old) RIG (CPA). DOUBLE Thanks FATHER!

87.   Chandra Levy (Rest In Glory) RIG (CPA no. 9)

(09 May 09) Sign Of 9's (out of seq.) Saturday: Finally an answer to my long-term prayer of (May 2001) the brutal slaying of Chandra Levy RIG in Washington D.C. Ingmar Guandique arrested and sentenced to death for the killing. (CPA) Thank you FATHER!

88.   Sandra Cantu (Rest In Glory) RIG (CPA no. 10)

(10 Apr 09) (out of seq.) Friday: Melissa Huckaby, grand-daughter of a Baptist minister in California arrested and charged with the murder of Sandra Cantu (8 years old) RIG; given the death penalty; her daughter was Sandra's playmate. (CPA) Thank you FATHER!

89.   Lana Clarkson (Rest In Glory) RIG (CPA no. 11)

(14 Apr 09) (out of seq.) Tuesday: Phil Spector, a well known record producer, found guilty of killing Lana Clarkson; an aspiring actress, he received (19 years to life in prison) for her brutal murder; this was the culmination of 6 years earnestly petitioning the HOLY SPIRIT, using my best weapon against crime; my novena (9 days of prayer) in the arsenal of GOD. (CPA) a BIG THANK'S on this one FATHER!

90.   Kathleen Peterson (Rest In Glory) RIG (CPA no. 12)

(07 May 09) (out of seq.) Thursday: Drew Peterson a former police officer, arrested for the brutal murder of 3rd wife Kathleen RIG by drowning her in the bathtub; gotten away with this for a very long time; I was praying constantly for his arrest and once again, as always, HOLY SPIRIT power prevails; there is no, "STATUE OF LIMITATIONS," ON MURDER. (CPA) Another TERRIFIC thanks for YOU, "ALMIGHTY GOD".

91.   Rodriguez Briant (Kidnapped But Safely Returned)

(16 May 09) (out of seq.) Saturday: I learned on this day, that a youngster (2 years old) male, named Rodriguez Briant, went missing; millions of children are missing every day and we, in our busy lives, are unaware of this evil in our mist. I sprang into action using my prayer weapon to the HOLY SPIRIT; he had been taken at gunpoint from his California home; GOD answered my petition and he was safely returned unharmed the very next day. (CPA) Thanks LORD!

92.   Naveah Buchanan (Rest In Glory) RIG (CPA no. 14)

(05 Jun 09) out of seq. Friday: This date would have been my 34th point, pearl or solution to my miracle function due to translation; but I must tell you that I don't care because I am holding back tears as I write these words; recalling the demise of a beautiful ANGEL OF GOD (5 years old) NEVAEH BUCHANAN, her mother named her by spelling HEAVEN backwards, when I heard that, I knew I had to pull out all stops to find her body; she was kidnapped off her scooter in her Detroit Michigan neighborhood; when I learned that her mother had been using her boyfriend, a dangerous offender as a male figure in her child's life; I wondered in my anger, "how could a mother be so stupid to allow this to happen?" I got down on my knees immediately and earnestly prayed, with all the fiber in my being, for the body location; the spirit answered (09 Jun 09) (Sign Of 9's) only FOUR days later. Two fisherman on a river bank, ONE using a concrete pad as a foot rest, while fishing, and my Heavenly Father, "GOD ALMIGHTY", split that concrete in two pieces; I know it was caused by the spirit's intervention and not the weight of the man's feet; under the concrete was the little body of Nevaeh; a shallow grave was her resting place, and the killers DNA was found on her remains; he had put her there hoping she would never be found; after he brutally raped and murdered her. The HOLY SPIRIT always permits evil to happen, for a much greater good; I even asked GOD, "where is that greater good, in a case of this nature"; we have to understand that this tragedy was caused by Satan NOT GOD; Satan is the author of all evil in the world; he

OWNS the world. JESUS said. "I am leaving for the ruler of this world is coming, but he has NO power over me; I will send you MY, "HOLY SPIRIT" to ward off Satan's attacks"; the Devil is trying, by this type of evil, to blame GOD"; we know that GOD is all GOOD and that HE can ONLY DO GOOD, and permit the evil in the world; because evil is the imperfection in nature, and nature belongs to the world, once owned by GOD, but now is the property of the world, the flesh and the devil himself. The much greater good is a part of GOD'S overall divine plan, which eventually will be in HIS timetable; now because of the power of the HOLY SPIRIT we will soon remove a dangerous monster from our streets. (CPA) A big thank you for our creator!

93.   "Suicide By Cop" (CPA no. 15)

(06 Jun 09) (out of seq.) Saturday: I prayed on this date to bring to justice, a spree killer in South Carolina; six victims were the result of this vicious psychopath and he needed to be apprehended immediately; he was killed in a, "suicide by cop", instance, the very next day in North Carolina. (CPA) Thanks as usual, to our Father In Heaven! Note: This event was a result of Satan's work and GOD put on the brakes.

94.   Hakimullah Mehsud (Potential WPA no. 2)

(06 Aug 09) (out of seq.) Thursday: After his wife was killed by drone, yesterday, a dangerous leader and terrorist, Mehsud, was also killed on this date in Pakistan; this was a (WPA) long over-due; THANKS LORD! (Note: Mehsud was implicated in the assassination of Benazir Bhutto in Pakistan) (Update flash: he is said to be still alive only wounded) (unverified at this time)

95.   Michael Jackson (Rest In Glory) RIG (CPA no.16)

(08 Feb 10) (out of seq.) Monday: Dr. Conrad Murray was finally arrested and ordered jailed, for manslaughter in the homicide case of Michael Jackson RIG; this was another prayer answered by "HOLY SPIRIT POWER"; I was on this case from (25 Aug 09), his passing on. (CPA) THANKS FATHER, another culprit brought to justice!

96.   Annie Le (Rest In Glory) RIG (CPA no.17)

(17 Sept 09) (out of seq.) Wednesday: A man named Clark the third, arrested and charged with the rape and murder of Annie Le (RIG), a grad student of Yale, on what was to be her wedding day; found in a wall in the lab where they worked together. THANKS LORD. (CPA) I received my answered prayer in only FOUR days.

97.   Somer Thompson (Rest In Glory) RIG (CPA no.18)

(19 Oct 09) (out of seq.) Monday: I'm sorry but I am crying again, because ANOTHER LITTLE ANGEL went to heaven, from her Florida neighborhood; her name, Somer Thompson (7 years old) RIG; she was kidnapped, raped, murdered and thrown in a dumpster and found in only two days, through mine and others, prayer intervention. THANKS TO
GOD, a man named Jarred Harell was arrested (26 Mar 10) and charged with 29 counts including possession of child porn. (CPA) THANK YOU FATHER FOR REMOVING THIS MONSTER FROM OUR STREETS!

98.   Morgan Harrington (Rest In Glory) RIG (CPA no.19)

(18 Oct 09) (out of seq.) Sunday: This case became one of my pet prayer projects, because this was the Morgan Harrington murder and as of late (01 Jul 10) a terrific break after three months of intensive petitions to the HOLY SPIRIT, not only did I need this, but the entire state of Virginia. The big break is a DNA link and criminal composite sketch of her killer; matching another murder in Fairfax, Virginia, 5 years ago. This hits home hard, because I live only 10 miles from the killing in 2005; I've been on this case since the get-go; and I won't rest until this psychopath is captured and given the death penalty; no morbid details are necessary here, except they were both raped and murdered brutally and just thrown away like a piece of trash. I'm now on my 51st novena (9 days of prayer in succession since September 2007) until I get my prayers answered and satisfied. That, my reader, is called perseverance on my part and confidence in GOD'S answer; because he says, "he will answer if we ask"; Morgan was a beautiful (20 year old) young lady and she and the other victim deserve, no

less than death penalty justice. THANKS FATHER FOR THE DNA MATCH AND COMPOSITE! (CPA) This isn't over yet, but I do expect justice before I complete and release this journal.

99.   Elizabeth Olten (Rest In Glory) RIG (CPA no.20)

(22 Oct 09) (out of seq.) Thursday: The good part of this case, involving the killing and shallow grave burial of(9 year old) Elizabeth Olten RIG in Missouri. is that her killer; a (15 year old) female juvenile led police to her body; and my prayers answered swiftly; she knew her and targeted her for murder, because she wanted to see what it was like to kill; a real psycho in my book; the bad part is the loss of such a beautiful young lady to the world. (CPA) THANKS FOR YOUR IMMEDIATE RESPONSE FATHER!

100.   Saeed (Killed, But Anwar Awlaki Escapes) (WPA no. 3)

(25 Dec 09) Christmas day (out of seq.) Friday: A wanted terrorist and dangerous leader of attacks in Pakistan, Saeed was killed by U.S. led Yemeni air-strike, but the real target, ANWAR AWLAKI; Hasan, responsible for attacks at Ft. Hood were linked to Awlaki, Awlaki escaped unharmed and is still at large, presumably in Yemen territory. I have been praying for a 2nd, this time successful strike. (WPA) For the Awlaki elimination. THANKS LORD! FLASH: Anwar Awlaki killed in mountains of Yemen (30 Sept 11).

101.   Mullah Brader Captured (WPA no. 4)

(15 Feb l0)(out of seq.)Monday: Mullah Brader, 2nd Taliban leader; 1st leader is Mullah Omar, captured in Karachi, Pakistan and interrogated giving up important information about the Taliban and its activities. (WPA) THANKS LORD! An important prayer answer; another bites the dust, with many to follow.

102.   Jason Williams Incarcerated (CPA no. 21)

(23 Feb l0) (out of seq.) Monday: Famous basketball star Jason Williams, finally brought to Justice for shooting his chauffeur RIG; getting away with it until my long term prayer as well as

other prayers from friends of the chauffeur, demanding justice were answered by the "HOLY SPIRIT POWER." CPA THANK YOU FATHER FOR GETTING HIM TO CONFESS TO MANSLAUGHTER; he received a sentence, 18 months minimum.

103.   Vehicle no. 2 (CPA no. 22)

(23 Mar 10) (out of seq.) Tuesday: I was in my 45th novena using my MOM's rosary to acquire another vehicle immediately; I only had one day (24 Mar 10) to return my leased
(2007 CTS) to GMAC leasing company. I invoked the HOLY SPIRITS intervention and he came through again with flying colors; very next day I was led to a waiting newer vehicle, which I called "Black Beauty"; 2009 Impala Chevy all in one-half day, that's GOD power. THANKS LORD! (CPA) (see effect no. 45 for more information)

104.   Chelsea King And Amber Dubois (Rest In Glory) RIG (CPA no. 23)

(02 Mar 10) (out of seq.) Tuesday: An early release in California of a dangerous prisoner named, Gardner the third proved to be a serious mistake, when two young women's remains were found in shallow graves, only six days apart; Chelsea King (17 years old) RIG and Amber Dubois (14 years old) RIG; he was convicted and sentenced to life without parole; I was praying for their killer to be caught since they went missing. (CPA) THANKS FATHER FOR REMOVING ANOTHER PSYCHO FROM OUR STREETS!

105.   "The King Of Heroin" Incarcerated (CPA no. 24)

(24 March 10) (out of seq.) Wednesday: Top drug King Pin called, "The King Of Heroin", by his criminal buddies, arrested in Mexico. (CPA) THANKS FATHER FOR ANSWERING MY PRAYERS TO GET THESE DRUG CARTEL LEADERS!

106.   Al-Masri And Al-Bacdadi Killed (WPA no. 5)

(19 Apr 10) (out of seq.) Monday. Two top Al Qaeda leaders killed in Iraq; Al-Masri an Al-Bacdadi, very dangerous terrorists brought

to swift justice by my "Hot Line to the HOLY SPIRIT" in full swing. (WPA) THAT'S, "GOD SERVICE", THANKS!

107.   Faisal A Domestic terrorist Arrested (WPA no. 6)

(03 May 10) (out of seq.) Saturday: Faisal, Domestic terrorist and would-be bomber, trained by Al Qaeda in Pakistan; arrested by the FBI in Times Square, N.Y. city. (WPA) THANKS FATHER! This would have been a disaster of epic proportions, had he carried out his plan successfully.

108.   Lawrence Taylor Scandal (CPA no. 25)

(07 May 10) (out of seq.) Friday: In the Lawrence Taylor's sex scandal, a popular pro-football player; man arrested for child sex trafficking of a (16 years old) runaway, who was prostituting herself for 300 dollars, for sex with Mr.Taylor. (CPA) THANKS FATHER for answering my each day morning prayers for bringing, especially, this type of criminal to justice; for human trafficking, a terrible evil in our society.

109.   Zeiden Killed (WPA no. 7)

(12 Jan 10) (out of seq.) Tuesday: Zeiden, an Al Qaeda leader in Jordan, killed by U.S. Drone in Pakistan. (WPA) THANKS LORD! WAR PRAYER ANSWERED.

110.   Militants (18 Killed This Week) (WPA no. 8)

(16 Jan 10) (out of seq.) Saturday: A total of (18) militants killed by Drone strike this week. (WPA) THANKS FATHER THAT'S REAL PROGRESS!

111.   Drug Dealer In Mexico Captured (CPA no. 26)

(17 Jan l0) (out of seq.) Sunday: One of the most Notorious wanted drug dealers captured in Mexico. (CPA) THANKS FATHER FOR TAKING THEM DOWN ONE AT A TIME!

112. Al-Qaeda in Yemen Killed (WPA no. 9)

(19 Jan 10) (out of seq.) Tuesday: Forces in Yemen kills Al Qaeda cell leader. (WPA) THANKS LORD, WE NEED ALL THE HELP WE CAN GET IN THIS TERRIBLE WAR!

113. Taliban Militants (12 Killed) (WPA no. 10)

(14 Jan 10) (out of seq.) Thursday: 12 Taliban killed by U.S. Drone strike in Pakistan, (WPA) THANKS AGAIN LORD!

114. Militants (15 Killed) (WPA no. 11)

(15 Jan 10) (out of seq.) Friday: U.S. Drone strike kills (15) in military camp in North Waziristan. (WPA) THANKS TO MY HEAVENLY FATHER!

115. Al-Raymi (Chief Of Yemeni Al-Qaeda Killed) (WPA no. 12)

(06 Jan 10) (out of seq.) Wednesday: Al-Raymi, chief of Yemeni Al Qaeda, killed, along with (6) militants in two vehicles, in northern country. (WPA) THANKS FOR ELIMINATION OF A TOP LEADER, LORD!

116. Militants Of Haqqani Network (3 Killed) (WPA no. 13)

(09 Jan 10) (out of seq.) Saturday: 4 U.S. missiles from a Drone, kills at least (3) more militants in North Waziristan of the Haqqani network who were hiding leaders and those responsible for (7) CIA killed in attack in east Afghanistan. (WPA) THANKS LORD FOR SELECTING SOME OF THE HAQQANI NETWORK to eliminate.

117. Al-Qaeda Fighters (3 Killed) (WPA no. 14)

(10 Jan 10) (out of seq.) Sunday: 3 Al Qaeda fighters killed by Yemeni forces. (WPA) THANK YOU LORD!

118. "Islamic Of Iraq" (Leader Arrested) (WPA no. 15)

(11 Jan 10) (out of seq.) Monday: Head of "Islamic Of Iraq", a terrorist attack leader, arrested in Iraq. (WPA) ONE day to ONE top terrorist at a time, LORD THANK YOU!

119. Militants (20 Killed) (WPA no. 16)

(18 Jan 10) (out of seq.) Monday: 20 militants killed, 12 were in North Waziristan, Pakistan. (WPA) THAT'S QUITE A DAYS WORK, THANKS FATHER!

120. Abdul Basit Usman Killed (WPA no. 17)

(21 Jan l0) (out of seq.) Thursday: Abdul Basit Usman, a Filipino terrorist and bomb making expert, with links to Abu Sayyaf a militant group; was killed by U.S. Drone strike in Pakistan. (WPA) I always ask GOD in my morning prayers, as opposed to my 3 p.m. afternoon novena's, to use the Drone as a tool and rain down upon our enemies fire and brimstone, similar to what he did to destroy Sodom and Gomorrah; in this case using missiles from the Drone. MY FATHER IN HEAVEN IS LISTENING AND ANSWERING!

121. Abu Kahuf Killed (WPA no. 18)

(22 Jun 10) (out of seq.) Friday: Abu Kahuf. an AI Qaeda leader responsible for bringing foreign fighters into the war, killed by U.S. and Iraqi Raid. (WPA) THANKS FATHER FOR KEEPING THIS TYPE OUT! We have enough to worry about, without this problem.

122. Militants (9 Killed) (WPA no. 19)

(30 Jun 10) (out of seq.) Saturday: 9 militants killed by U.S. Drone strike in Pakistan. (WPA) THANKS LORD! Your wonderful and almighty.

123. Members Of Haqqani Network (17 killed) (WPA no. 20)

(02 Feb l0) (out of seq.) Tuesday: 17 members of the Haqqani network, a very elusive and dangerous group believed dead by U.S.

Drone strike in North Waziristan, Pakistan. (WPA) THANKS FATHER! The network plans attack everywhere and as mentioned before, even members of the CIA.

124. Militants (3 Killed) (WPA no. 21)

(18 Feb 10) (out of seq.) Thursday: 3 militants killed by U.S. air strike in North Waziristan. (WPA) THANK YOU FATHER! You always answer if we ask.

125. Mohammad Haqqani Killed (WPA no. 22)

(19 Feb l0) (out of seq.) Friday: Mohammed Haqqani, one of six sons of leader Jalaluddin Haqqani killed by U.S. Drone strike in Pakistan. (WPA) THANKS FATHER! Now go after the remaining five sons.

126. Militants (30 Killed) (WPA no. 23)

(20 Feb 10) (out of seq.) Saturday: 30 militants killed in South Waziristan by Pakistan air force jets. (WPA) THANKS LORD! Hit them where we find them in those hidden and difficult tribal regions.

127. Parad Killed (WPA no. 24)

(21 Feb 10) (out of seq.) Sunday: Parad, one of the most wanted leaders, for 10 years, of Abu Sayyaf militant group in the Philippines, killed today. (WPA) THANKS LORD! They can run but they can't hide, when prayer power is on their tail.

128. Hajizaman Ghamshark Killed (WPA no. 25)

(22 Feb 10) (out of seq.) Monday: Hajìzaman Ghamshark, one of the most wanted Taliban leaders killed; he was close to Bin Laden; he helped him escape at Tora Bora; when we thought we had him cornered. (WPA) THANK YOU FATHER! WE'RE GETTING CLOSER TO PAYDIRT.

129. Taliban Leader captured (WPA no. 26)

(23 Feb 10) (out of seq.) Tuesday: A Taliban leader captured at the, "Battle of Marjah" in Afghanistan. (WPA) THANK YOU FATHER! This was a successful operation, next target being Kandahar.

130. Militants (4 Killed) (WPA no. 27)

(24 Feb 10) (out of seq.) Wednesday: 4 militants killed by U.S. Drone strike in North Waziristan. (WPA) THANKS FOR ANSWERING FATHER! These are important too.

131. Zarfar Killed (WPA no. 28)

(25 Feb 10) (out of seq.) Thursday: Zarfar, killed; responsible for the assassination of a wonderful Pakistani leader Benizer Bhutto RIG, utilizing a homicide bomber. (WPA) THANKS LORD! It's nice to eliminate the big one's and receive justice for such a wonderful soul; he had a 5 million bounty in U.S.

132. Fighter (56 Killed) (WPA no.29)

(17 May 10) (out of seq.) Monday: 56 fighters killed in Northern Pakistan. (WPA) THANKS TO YOU FATHER! A big hit this time.

133. Al-Qahtani Killed Accidently (WPA no.30)

(21 May 10) (out of seq.) Friday: Al-Qahtani, a leader of Al Qaeda in the Arab Peninsula, accidently killed while playing with a bomb he was making. (WPA) THANKS FATHER! Answered prayers are not accidents.

134. Militants (9 Killed) (WPA no. 31)

(22 May 10) My 73rd Birthday (out of seq.) Saturday: 9 militants killed by Drone strike in Pakistan. (WPA) THANKS HOLY SPIRIT! A nice 73rd birthday present for your servant!

135. Jan (Second To The Taliban Leader Mullah Omar) (WPA no. 32)

(04 Mar 10) (out of seq.) Thursday: Jan, a political Tatiban leader in Karachi, arrested in Pakistan; he is 2nd to Mullah Omar, the big cheese. (WPA) THANKS FATHER FOR THIS ANSWER, and go after the top next; he's well hidden.

136. Top Commanders (3 captured) and Taliban (30 Killed) (WPA no. 33)

(05 Mar 10) (out of seq.) Friday: 30 Tailban killed and 3 top commanders, so called, "Money Men" captured in Afghanistan. (WPA) THANKS LORD! We also need to disrupt their financial network.

137. Maulvi Mohammad (Close Friend Of Bin Laden) (WPA no. 34)

(06 Mar 10) (out of seq.) Saturday: Maulvi Mohammad, a close friend of Bin Laden and Al Zawahiri and a top commander in Pakistan, killed in air-strike. (WPA) THANKS FATHER FOR THE PRAYER ANSWERED! We are skimming the top.

138. Al-Ada, Aza Captured(WPA no. 35)

(07 Mar 10) (out of seq.) Sunday: Al-Adam Aza, an American Muslim of the Mujahdeen, captured. (WPA) THANKS LORD! We are after them all with prayer power.

139. Militants (10 Killed) (WPA no. 36)

(08 Mar 10) (out of seq.) Monday: 10 militants killed in Pakistan and Philippines in combination. (WPA) THANKS FATHER! Will take them in combinations when necessary.

140. Militants (6 Killed) (WPA no. 37)

(10 Mar 10) (out of seq.) Wednesday: 6 militants killed by U.S. Drone strike in North Waziristan. (WPA) AS BEFORE, THANKS AGAIN FATHER FOR YOUR SPIRITS INTERVENTION!

141.   Militants (16 Killed) (WPA no. 38)

(14 Mar 10) (Out of seq.) Sunday: 16 militants killed in North Waziristan by Pakistan air-strike and 3 hideouts destroyed. (WPA) THANKS LORD! They can't hide from the spirit rath.

142.   Commanders Of Al-Qaeda (2 Killed) (Yemen Strike) (WPA no. 39)

(15 Mar 10) (out of seq.) Monday: Two members of Al Qaeda, both commanders, killed in Yemen air-strike. (WPA) THANKS AGAIN FATHER! We get the top dogs when we locate them with spy satellites.

143.   Militants (11 Killed, 2 Wounded) (WPA no. 40)

(16 Mar 10) (out of seq.) Tuesday. 11 militants killed by U.S. Drone and 2 wounded in North Waziristan. (WPA) THANKS TO "HOLY SPIRIT PRAYER POWER"! Once we locate them, we eliminate them.

144.   Members of Al-Qaeda Arrested In Saudi Arabia (WPA no. 41)

(24 Mar 10) (out of seq.) Wednesday: 113 members of Al Qaeda arrested in Saudi Arabia. (WPA) A BIG THANK YOU FATHER! Our friends also are intervening to help with this enormous undertaking; a large number down the drain.

145.   Sadam Al-Hussami Killed (WPA no. 42)

(17 Mar 10) (out of seq.) Wednesday- Sadam Al-Hussami; a significant blow was delivered to terror networks, when he was killed today, (WPA) YOUR ON THE JOB SPIRIT! THANKS FROM YOUR SERVANT.

146.   Hussein Al-Yemeni Of Al-Qaeda killed (WPA no. 43)

(18 Mar 10) (out of seq.) Thursday: Hussein Al-Yemeni, top Al Qaeda leader, killed by U.S. Drone strike in Pakistan. (WPA) THANKS TO "HOLY SPIRIT PRAYER POWER"! Eventually we'll get all top leaders, through patience and perseverance.

147. Militants (6 Killed) (WPA no. 44)

(30 Mar 10) (out of seq.) Tuesday: 6 militants killed by U.S. Drone strike in North Waziristan. (WPA) THANK YOU LORD FOR GIVING ME PATIENCE IN MY NOVENA PRAYERS! Even THIS small sum is significant.

148. Homicide Bombers (7 Killed By Afghans) (2 Arrested) (WPA no. 45)

(05 May 10) (out of seq.) Wednesday: 7 homicide bombers, killed by Afghans and 2 arrested. (WPA) THANKS SPIRIT! They can't hide from your power, even when they disguise themselves as WOMEN.

149. Militants (24 Killed) (WPA no. 46)

(10 May 10) (out of seq.) Monday: 24 militants killed by U.S. Drone strike in North Waziristan near the Afghan Border. (WPA)

150. Father Jack Burial Date (4 Militants Killed) (WPA no. 47)

(12 May 10) (out of seq.) Wednesday: Recall this date as the burial date of my beloved, Father Jack Fullen (RIG) (see effect no. 1B): 4 militants killed by U.S Drone strike in Pakistan. (WPA) THANKS FATHER!

151. Mullah Zergay Killed (Was Taliban Leader) (WPA no. 48)

(31 May 10)(out of seq.) Memorial day Monday: Mullah Zergay, a Taliban leader, who planned attacks, killed in Kandahar, Afghanistan. (WPA) THANKS LORD! This was a big hit.

152. Mustafa Abu Al-Yazid (Founder Of Al-Qaeda) (WPA no. 49)

(01 Jun 10) out of seq. Tuesday: Sheikh Sa'id Al-Masri, ANA, MustafaAbu Al-Yazid, no. 3 leader and founder of Al Qaeda a top commander and chief of operations, killed by U.S. Drone strike in Pakistan. (WPA) This demonstrates, "HOLY SPIRIT PRAYER POWER" to it's utmost; one of the best eliminations we've had so far; a VERY BIG THANKS TO MY FATHER IN HEAVEN! This was marvelous.

153. Joran Van Dersloot (Kills Again, Arrested In Peru) (CPA no. 27)

(03 Jun 10) (out of seq.) Thursday: Joran Van Dersloot arrested and is in custody and confessed, I'm sorry but I'm crying again as I write this; the psychopath killer from Aruba strikes again killing, another beautiful young girl Stephanie Flores Ramerez in Peru; she was found in his hotel room strangled, broken neck and beaten, presumably by his fists. Evidently he never changed his tactic's and lying, about Natalie Holloway's murder; or when my Father In Heaven; took his father last year; on a tennis court with a heart attack; I know his father IS IN HELL because he covered up Natalie's murder; and certainly, you don't think that he would be allowed in Heaven, where Natalie is a Saint do you? I had followed this killer since I've known about him; prayed for his capture, with every fiber of my being; my Heavenly Father answered; but I wasn't happy to see another tragedy of this magnitude. (CPA) THANKS TO YOU LORD! He will never have the chance to kill again.

154. Texas Man Connected To Al-Anwar Awlaki (Arrested) (WPA no. 50)

(04 Jun 10) (out of seq.) Friday: A Texas man, who contacted Al-Anwar Awlaki; the radical cleric from America and now escaped to Yemen; a bounty on his head; was arrested for terrorism and helping Al Qaeda. (WPA) THANK YOU FATHER!

155. Taliban Fighters (13 Killed) (WPA no. 51)

(10 Jun 10) (out of seq.) Thursday: 13 Taliban fighters killed by U.S. Drone strike in North West Pakistan. (WPA) THANKS LORD!

156. Drug Cartel Leader (Arrested) (CPA no. 28)

(11 Jun 10) (out of seq.) Friday: A notorious drug cartel leader arrested in Mexico. (CPA) THANK YOU FATHER! Even the big boys can't get away.

157. Militants (13 Killed) (WPA no. 52)

(19 Jun l0) (out of seq.) Saturday: At least 13 more militants killed by U.S. Drone strike in North West Pakistan. (WPA) THANKS TO, "HOLY SPIRIT PRAYER POWER"!

158. Additional Words Needed For The Journal (CPA no. 29)

(20 Jun 10) Fathers day (out of seq.) Sunday: My prayers to the "HOLY SPIRIT" were answered on this appropriate date; I had asked for additional words to be used to fuel this journal; the answer being, "use my list of people", thus I knew how to continue this journey. (CPA) THANKS FATHER FOR THAT ANSWER!

159. Christopher Dudas Coke (World's Worst Drug Dealer) (Arrested) (CPA no. 30)

(24 Jun 10) (out of seq.) Thursday: Christopher Dudus Coke, one of the most dangerous drug lords in the world, arrested in Jamaica to be extradited to the U.S. (CPA) THANKS FATHER! On this date, "The Celebration Of The Nativity Of St. John The Baptist"!

160. Fake Woman Taliban Woman Killed (WPA no. 53)

(26 Jun 10) (out of seq.) Saturday: A Taliban commander disguised as a woman SHOT DEAD. (WPA) THANKS LORD! They can try all tactics, but we are too intelligent for their shenanigans.

161. Nina's Link With My Near-Death Experience AT&T Her Company (CPA no. 31)

(03 May 10) (out of seq.) Monday: I had asked the HOLY SPIRIT to put a special woman in my path; I was led to Martine in the morning and Nina in the afternoon, both considered now my special Angels; THANK YOU FOR ANSWERING ONE OF MY MOST IMPORTANT PETITIONS ON THIS TREK THROUGH TIME! (CPA) (see effect no. 52 and 53) ALSO: NINA told me that her company AT&T's customers phone service

number 611 is identical to my miracle bible no. 611; again showing she is DEFINITELY linked to my near-death experience.

162. Taliban Commander Captured (WPA no. 54)

(09 Jul 10) (back in seq.) Monday: A Taliban commander, responsible for bringing militants into Afghanistan to launch attacks; a member of the notorious group called, "LET" who carried out the Atrocities at Mumbai, India; captured by NATO and Afghan troops. (WPA) THANKS AGAIN, AND AGAIN FOR, "HOLY SPIRIT PRAYER POWER", AMEN!!

163. Jack Nolan's Wife's Cancer In Remission (CPA no. 32)

(24 Jul 10) Saturday: I spoke with Jack Nolan after 9 a.m. mass today and asked him, "how is your wife, since I gave him a first draft copy of my journal and his wife dominated
the reading", he told me, "since she had cancer; he also informed me, she is in FULL REMISSION NOW and her prognosis is excellent"; going to my miracle calendar again I found this date would have been my 35th point, pearl or solution to my miracle equation (Y1=70); because this date falls directly on a Tuesday when one translates it from (2010) to (2007). TRULY a BLESSING from the FATHER! (CPA)

164. A Friend Of Mine (Cancer Cleared) (CPA no. 33)

(26 Jul 10) Monday: My friend informed me today that he went to the hospital to have a Biopsy on his face of squamous cell skin cancer; I had told him that I put him on my novena prayer list, ever since I gave him a partial first draft copy of my journal when we met (27 Nov 09); he had some skepticism, as many people do; it's natural; but the prognosis of his skin cancer is GREAT NEWS; he was told and they found in the Biopsy the cancer has cleared, meaning NO cancer cells are present; VOILA! HOLY SPIRIT PRAYER POWER SURFACES AGAIN (CPA); ADDITIONALLY recall the true statement I made in the preface of this journal; it is emphatic and must be repeated here; "there are NO coincidences in life ONLY STEPS IN GOD'S PLAN"; this is TRULY an ACT OF GOD; consulting my miracle calendar

once again, I discovered; this date (26 Jul 10) would have been my 36th point, pearl or solution to my miracle equation (Y1='70); it falls on a Thursday IDENTICAL TO effect no. 14 (see graphics effect no. 30) when ONE, AGAIN translates this date from (2010 to 2007); another DOUBLE-WHAMMY; meaning, TWO concentric circles around "26" on my miracle calendar; THANK YOU HEAVENLY FATHER! All readers of this journal should rejoice; this proves miracles do happen in our world, today; he has been healed COMPLETELY and ABSOLUTELY of this horrible disease, caused by Satan, NOT GOD; remember, GOD is ALL GOOD and can't do evil; HE rewarded him for his courage.

165. Shaker Masri (26 Years Old Chicago Man Arrested) (WPA no. 55)

(04 Aug 10) Wednesday: A 26 year old Chicago man was arrested and charged with attempting to aid Al Qaeda Shaker Masri was unaware that an FBI informant was his new companion and told him, "he planned to go to Somalia to help the terrorist group and asked him for money to buy guns, once he got there" and also that, "he hoped to become a Martyr by wearing a suicide vest"; Masri is a U.S. citizen born in Alabama but raised Abroad. (WPA) THANKS FATHER! No matter who you are or what you are; you can't escape GOD'S wrath; actually HOLY SPIRIT intervention may have saved Masri from eternal punishment in hell; HOW IRONIC!

166. Message no 24. (Spirit Prompt) (GOD's Glory, Electrum Verified)

(09 Aug 10) Monday: This date is very important; not only is this a continuing, "Sign Of 9's"; but during mass this morning I detected the SAME JOY as I experienced on (09 Jan 07); my time in the 7th dimension of eternity; because the reading at mass was, EZEKIEL CHAPTER 1; when he was given the vision of GOD on HIS sapphire throne above the cherubim; depicting GOD as having (from my miracle bible no. 611 I quote "the appearance of a man upward from what resembled his waist, I saw what gleamed like ELECTRUM; an alloy of gold and silver; downward from what resembled HIS waist, I saw what looked like

fire; he was surrounded with splendor, like the bow which appears in the clouds on a rainy day was the splendor that surrounded HIM; such was the vision of the likeness of the Glory Of The Lord." I know I witnessed a portion of "GOD'S GLORY" when I encountered, "The Dome Of Creation" that wonderful January morning; it was from indeed, NOT gold suspended from the apex of the Dome; but I am certain now, more than ever; it was ELECTRUM; the HOLY SPIRIT himself revealing to me just a snippet of our Heavenly Fathers majesty, power and awesome Glory; THANKS GOD FOR THIS REMEMBRANCE OF MY 3RD ANNIVERSARY OF MY 4TH MIRACLE OF THE DOME. (see effect no. 18) Additionally, this fact must be noted here: I never would have realized the importance of this date had it not been for the joyful "SPIRIT ALERT", I received during mass; my 24th message; a vision of GOD given to the Prophet Ezekiel and analogous to "The Dome Of The Sky" Genesis reading (see corroboration effect no. 3) on this very same day I met Father Jack Fullen (21 Apr 07) when I was bewildered by the amazing events that were happening to me on a daily basis; of course, the two readings established a definite link to his correct explanation of my near-death experience; my continuing journey in conformance with GOD'S WILL for me.

167.   Elias Abuelazam (Israeli Man) Arrested (CPA no. 34)

(12 Aug 10) Thursday: Elias Abuelazam, a (33 year old lsraely man) was finally arrested today, he was dubbed the "Serial Stabber" and malice murderer responsible for 18 random attacks, of which 5 died in Flint Michigan and others were wounded in 3 different states; Michigan, Virginia and Toledo Ohio; all victims were African American, this was definitely racially motivated, he was attempting to board a plane bound for Tel Aviv, Israel, when he was apprehended, I along with millions of others had been praying for his immediate capture, when we learned these victims were randomly selected. (CPA) HOLY SPIRIT PRAYER POWER NEVER FAILS; this case demonstrates a basic philosophical truth I learned in "Philosophical Psychology", the philosophy of man; that man tends to the GOOD, but is Basically EVIL; this type of person is definitely motivated by invisible Satanic prompts;

similar to, "Son Of Sam" (David Berkawitz) Ted Bundy, the freeway killers, and other serial murders; THANKS FATHER! For removing another dangerous predator from our mist and making it safer for us to walk the streets again.

168.   Stryker Brigade (Last Combat Team To Leave Iraq) (WPA no. 56)

(19 Aug 10) Thursday: A milestone was reached today when the whole world was able to see "The Last Stryker Brigade" of combat type soldiers, leaving Iraq behind, after seven years of successful liberating endeavors; it was broadcast live on national TV; a very special day indeed, because of this event I, and millions of others prayers were answered. (WPA) THANKS AGAIN FATHER; "how truly great thou art"; this links directly to my near-death experience because I intensified my morning prayers; of which this played a significant role and the LORD came through and rewarded me for my patience and perseverance of this long-term request.

169.   Meeting no. 3 With Martine

(21 Aug 10) Saturday: I was caught completely by surprise today, to my delight, when I was leaving my customary 9:00 a.m. mass; I again ran into (our 3rd meeting) a very special lady; Martine, (see effect no. 71); she exhibited a beautiful smile and embraced me; saying she loved my partial first draft copy I gave her of the journal and also its companion the no. 611 miracle bible; a stark contrast of her behavior at our very FIRST meeting; both rejoiced and acknowledged the "HOLY SPIRITS" responsibility for this encounter; I couldn't wait to go home and add this positive feedback to the journal; I also almost overlooked another important fact: this date (21 Aug 10) would have produced another DOUBLE-WHAMMY; meaning, TWO concentric circles around "21" on my miracle calendar and also would have been my 37th point, pearl or solution to my miracle equation (Y1=70); it falls on a Tuesday, IDENTICAL to effect no. 43 (see graphics effect no. 30) when translating the year (2010 back to 2007) once again demonstrating the "HOLY SPIRITS POWER AND MYSTERIOUS VERSATILITY"; in the usage of this journal as

another inspirational tool of conversion; in this case for the benefit of Martine and her 17 year old daughter Anne (see effect no. 53) for Martine's obvious transformation.

170. Message no. 25 (Spirit Prompt) "A Joyful Exercise For The Soul"

(22 Aug 10) I received my 25th message on a PROMPT FROM SPIRIT at 2:30 a.m. this morning; as I lay awake wondering why it had been such a long time where I hadn't received an overwhelming joyful experience; the answer was immediate; I had this power of joy from the spirit in my hands all the time and didn't realize it until now; the spirit taught me this exercise; told me to call it "A JOYFUL EXERCISE FOR THE SOUL" also to teach it to others as follows: cup both hands with palms facing you; bring them together so the smallest fingers are touching each other; then both hands which are now together; facing you, are raised to your forehead with palms in contact with the forehead while your fingers of both hands are in contact with only the top of your head; then the spirit continued; with light pressure, move your two hands over your face in a downward direction; then each hand separately over the sides of your body in a somewhat rapid motion, all the while maintaining equal pressure until your maximum reach is established in a lying, face-up position and from the very beginning of the exercise repeating the following words: "HOLY SPIRIT,

BLESSED MOTHER, YOU ARE THE CAUSE OF MY JOY"; when limited reach occurs, spread each arm out wide as if you are embracing the spirit or similar to your suspension from a cross; the more rapidly you move your hands down both sides of your body, increasing the pressure each time, the greater your joy should be; I did it, and the spirit was correct, for I almost became breathless with the increased joy I was experiencing during seven to nine rapid cycles; I was told, "this procedure is similar to the laying on of hands, for healing; the only difference being, one is using one's own body instead of another's, and joy; in some cases maybe healing as well, depending on the individuals reason for performing the exercise; this is a free gift (A PEARL) from our Heavenly Fathers infinite love for us, use it often.

171.   Message no. 26 (Spirit Prompt) Vehicle For Felicia

(26 Aug 10) Thursday: My special Angel Nina called and said, "her daughter Felicia (22 years old) was in a small crisis"; she needed a car by Monday (30 Aug 10) to commute to her senior year at Morgan University; from Washington DC. To Baltimore; a distance of 37 miles everyday she is graduating next year in the field of communications and will be employed with a TV station in Washington and she recently had a baby boy; I was in the process of completing my 55th novena (9 days of prayer) with my mother's rosary, when I remembered what "HOLY SPIRIT PRAYER POWER" had accomplished only 5 months before, in March (see effect no. 45) in regards to being led to my car; so I was moved by the spirit, immediately to contact that same dealer; Pallone Chevrolet and Magic; the nickname of my salesman; he told me he had one (2005) Malibu Classic for sale with 84k miles; I said I wouldn't be able to see it until Saturday morning; but the HOLY SPIRIT, had other ideas and I received an urgent message (no. 26) as follows: "GO NOW"!! When I arrived at the dealer, Magic had the door open on the vehicle with air conditioning running; it was a beautiful 4 door Sedan, silver, a perfect car for Felicia, I was astonished; in the span of 5 months and a total elapsed time of the purchase of two fine cars of only 4 hours; I considered this result as 2 gifts, (Pearls) from the HOLY SPIRIT; mine and Felicia's vehicle; most readers may call this luck but in light of my post-evidence of 44 months. Now; I know this to be GODS work.

172.   Cynthia's Miracle (Personal Banker)

(30 Aug 10) Monday: I was in the process of applying for an equity line of credit, greater than I had originally at a different bank in 2007; praying to the "HOLY SPIRIT" about this, when I met a personal banker named Cynthia; I was prompted to ask her, "if she believes in miracles", my standard opening acquaintance comment; she said, "she did", and proceeded to tell me about a miracle that happened in Peru between her and her mother when she was a young woman; I discovered she was also a Catholic; she began, "I was with my mom swimming in the ocean, we were alone, all of a sudden a RIP current caught us both and we were in trouble and

my mother was swept away and I was unable to rescue her and my mother drowned, because the RIP current was too strong; I was left all alone fighting for my life needless to say I was terrified; and about to drown in deep water about (5) blocks from dry land; all of a sudden something lifted me from the peril I was in, and I woke up safely on dry land; it must have been my Guardian Angel or the HOLY SPIRITS intervention that saved me that day"; I was looking at a "WALKING MIRACLE", across her desk; another near-death experience linking me to others aforementioned in this journal; remember (see effect no. 2 Margot; effect no. 14) morning show with two near-death experiences; see effect no. 50 Jennifer; effect no. 43 Jim; effect no. 49 Judy; effect no.51 Donna, all because of leads from the spirit; gifts, pearls, points or solutions to miracle equation (Y1=70); NOW add the 38th Pearl to the string; because this date (30 Aug 10) falls on a Thursday, when translated from 2010 back to 2007; additionally; I know at this point in my journey that I will obtain the credit line I am applying for in 4-6 weeks from today; I have that assurance, as I did when I received my first line on my home in (Oct 2007) that my heavenly Father will answer my request; by the way; Cynthia and I compared our experiences and she gave me her phone number, to call her when I released the journal for publication.

173.   Meeting no. 2 With Father Daniel's 2nd Visit To Nativity

(06 Sept 10) Monday: This was a great day because another "DOUBLE-WHAMMY", two concentric circles around "6" on my miracle calendar; 2 pearls are given to me (no. 39 and 40 as gifts from, "THE HOLY SPIRIT"; when this date is translated back to 2007, it falls on a Thursday, more points, Pearls and solutions for (Y1=70); it occurred in this manner; I met Father Daniel (see effect no. 27 and 59) for the 2nd time visiting Nativity; he accepted 22 pages of this journal to take back with him to Africa and blessed me for the 2nd time also asking me to pray for him again; I complied with his request because he always believed in me and the Dome miracle; that equals pearl no. 39 and 40, involved my special Angel Nina; because on this date, she started a new life, a better home for visits from her grown children and the

furniture she selected was delivered; this may not be significant for my readers, but to Nina it was a GOD send PEARL.

174.   My FICO Credit Score Exceeds Maximum (Sign Of 9's)

(09 Sept 10) Thursday: This turned out to be a fantastic day; not only is the Sign Of 9's apparent, meaning, Sept being the 9th month and on the 9th day of the month this marks my 44th month since my near-death experience and to top that, pearl no. 41 is given to me in a letter I received from my bank involving my higher equity line of credit application; my FICO credit score exceeded my previous score in 2007; going from 755 to 860. THANK YOU HOLY SPIRIT!

175.   Bishop David Zubik's Healing And Sarah Shroud Released (CPA no. 35 And CPA no.36)

(13 Sept 10) Monday: This turned out to be another, "HUMDINGER" of a day: another "DOUBLE-WHAMMY" generating 2 pearls (no. 42 and 43) two concentric circles around "13" on my miracle calendar; pearl no. 42 is due to my prayer being answered (CPA) for Bishop David Zubik healing of a liver illness he had for several weeks (I don't know how serious it was) (see effect no. 63); pearl no. 43 is given to me also in "HOLY SPIRIT PRAYER POWER" fashion; by answering my morning prayer for at least ONE of the captive American hiker's of the 3 being held in Iran; SARAH SHROUD was released; of course translating this date (13 Sept 10) from 2010 to 2007, falls on a Thursday 2 more points or pearls, solutions to the miracle equation ($YI'=70$) remember, I'm only demonstrating here how rapidly this straight line equation or "String Of Pearls" in the VERNACULAR of the "HOLY SPIRIT"; is moving through time, approaching infinity or eternity (as the case may be), while the occurrence probability has always been equal to ZERO, when only 5 points, pearls combinations were calculated; this further shows the power of the supreme being.

176.   Ninth Anniversary Of 9/11 NY Tragedy

(11 Sept 10) Saturday: This was a very interesting day; not only was it the 9th anniversary of the tragedy caused by Satan, in the deliberate, devastating attack on our country by Al Qaeda, but the 911 links to my near-death experience (see effect no. 37) generates 2 pearls (no. 44 and 45) another "DOUBLE-WHAMMY", two concentric circles around "11" on my miracle calendar; these Pearls no. 44 and 45, occurred as follows; I was returning from a prayer visit before 5 p.m. mass, at the "Lady Of Fatima" statue in Nativity park, when I was led off the main path to the parking area, presumably by the spirit, to a young lady sitting at a picnic table; I approached her introducing myself and began our acquaintance; her name was SASHA; looked to be in her early twenties; asked, "if she believed in miracles", and she did, but she wasn't Catholic (she was from the Ukraine) we discussed my near-death experience and she of course wanted more details of the Dome experience; to which I had complied; she told me, "she wasn't sure what profession she wanted to pursue in college"; but thought seriously about the field of medicine, a Pediatrician; I said, "go for it"; she gave me her phone number and said to contact her; this was given to me as a pearl no. 45; when this date involving the Sign Of 9's, meaning, 9th anniversary of 911 is translated from 2010 to 2007, 3 concentric circles are apparent, because (1) circle was already there; but that pearl, point was already established as stated above; Sasha asked me to pray for her vocation the HOLY SPIRIT see's for her; I did; she works as an "Au Pair" and is very difficult to contact. I learned later she returned to the Ukraine.

177.   Declaration Of Miracle In The Catholic Church (cardinal John Neuman) (First American Saint)

(15 Sept 10) Wednesday: I was all set today to watch my favorite daytime show at 2 p.m. this afternoon when a PROMPT FROM SPIRIT caused me to tune in Fox SATV at 1:15 p.m. instead; I was led to a news flash regarding the Catholic church declaring a miracle involving a man who had for years been unable to stand up straight; a very painful and chronic condition of curvature of the spine known as Scoliosis; he had been praying to GOD through the 19th century English Cardinal John Neuman and was

completely healed to his doctors astonishment and bewilderment of the dramatic straightening of his spine; to which they had NO sufficient explanation; calling it a miracle; the man was on national TV and said, "he felt heat in the lower back area and all of a sudden was able to stand up straight" that's his only explanation; the church had investigated this potential miracle for a long time, attributing it to John Neuman and beatified him due to his intervention at this time; beatification in the Catholic church is the FIRST step necessary for Cardinal Neuman to be canonized, meaning, to declare a deceased person an officially recognized Saint; since I was led to this event by the spirit; this becomes pearl no. 46; simply because it is a significant supernatural event; a miracle was declared after extensive and meticulous investigation using ecclesiastical law; also this date falls in the "Plane Of Pearls" linked to my near-death experience of the miracle equation (Yl=70).

178.   Reconciliation (With Cookie)

(18 Sept 10) Saturday: I met a woman at 9 am. mass today; I hadn't seen in 3 years since 2007 from my neighborhood church; St. Raymonds, where this journey through time began; her name was Cookie (a nickname); to show you the power of the Spirit of GOD; she once wasn't very fond of me; but today she beckoned to me and I approached her cautiously and she gave me a big hug to my surprise; I proceeded to tell her about the journal; she already knew of my 2007 experiences from our initial acquaintances at St. Raymonds; she wished me luck with a big smile I had never seen on her face before; saying she loved me; she had changed for the good, as we all do as we gracefully age; we learn the hard way; so this generates pearl no. 47, because of our unexpected reconciliation; besides; this date falls on a Tuesday when translated from 2010 back to 2007; adding another solution, point, pearl, to my miracle equation (Y1=70) now we are very good friends again; thanks to the HOLY SPIRITS power present in my life today and forever.

179. Nina's Potential new career (Own Business And Neuman A saint) Killer captured (CPA no. 37)

(20 Sept 10) Monday: My first "TRIPLE-WHAMMY" (3 concentric circles around "20" on my miracle calendar) happened today, meaning, 3 prayers answered in one day; certainly significant as follows: Pearl no. 48 is due to Cardinal Neuman being officially declared the first American Saint in Heaven; Pearl no. 49 due to Nina's beginning of the fulfillment of her dreams, a lease agreement for her own business (rather than working for someone else); a potential perfect store setting, with kitchen facilities; Pearl no. 50 is a (CPA); the North Carolina's police chief's daughter's killer was captured in one day; this was my morning prayer answered as soon as I heard the tragedy, the previous day; thanks once again to, "HOLY SPIRIT PRAYER POWER"; I had been very angry that such evil could take place.

180. Bonnie's Mother (90 Years Old) Cleared Of Breast Cancer (CPA no. 38)

(23 Sept 10) Thursday: I was told today that the mother of Nina's friend Bonnie, who I met only 4 months ago, being 90 years old at the time, was found to have a tumor in one breast; Bonnie said to pray for her mom, because she had refused to have any treatment, whatsoever; I added her to my morning prayer list, as opposed to my 3 p.m. novena list; I'm happy to report that GOD answered our prayers (CPA) for she has been cleared of all cancer. PRAISE GOD! "HOLY SPIRIT PRAYER POWER" is on the job; this of course generates pearl no. 51 due to its certain significance but I don't know the circumstances of the diagnosis and because its math coordinate would lie in the plane of the 2007 link to my near-death experience if I needed additional verification; therefore I can't deem this a miracle; but with Heavenly certainty I can say it is an answered petition from our FATHER.

181. Edwin (Spirit Led me To A Despondent Man)

(25 Sept 10) Saturday: I was early for the 5 p.m. Vigil mass so I decided to pray at "Our Lady Of Fatima Statue" at Nativity park; I was sitting after prayers quietly on a bench, when I noticed a young man approaching the middle bench and sat down with his

head down and he began sobbing uncontrollably; he said, "his name was Edwin"; I went to him and put my left arm over his shoulder to console him; he said his wife had just left him and he was despondent; I told him about my near-death experience of 2007 and he listened intently and stopped crying; a smile replaced the sadness he was feeling and we got acquainted; I asked him if he would like to attend mass with me and he said yes; I knew the spirit had brought us together, because he could have harmed himself there all alone; our paths crossed purposely; we went to mass and received communion and he said, "he and his wife were married by Father Wilson, who was saying this mass"; after mass he shook hands with Father Wilson who had believed me for 3 years since I became a member of Nativity Parish when I was led to Nativity by the "HOLY SPIRIT"; Edwin acknowledged him and we all smiled; Father was told by Edwin that his wife walked out; he was surprised to hear such bad news; immediately he blessed Edwin and consoled him, as I took Edwin into the gift shop and showed him my miracle bible no. 611 and the "Dome Of Creation" illustration on page 5 of Genesis; his eyes widened and he asked me if he could purchase one; I told him I could get a better price at "Paschal Lamb" in Fairfax; he said to get him one and he would reimburse me next Saturday: I said, "everything would get better and for him to pray to the spirit for his wife's return"; he said he would; then he confessed to me, it was totally his fault, but he had repented and GOD had forgiven him, but his wife didn't buy it, so she's still not ready to forgive him; I said, "it is going to take an intervention by GOD through prayer and some counseling by Father Wilson, to reunite them again"; he accepted my advice and we left as new friends; he promised to heed my suggestions and to use the no.611 bible as another tool in GOD'S arsenal; this date and circumstances constitute pearl no. 52, because translating back to 2007 from 2010 (25 Sept 10) falls on a Tuesday on my miracle calendar, an additional, point, pearl, solution to (Yl=70).

182.   New credit Line Approved (CPA no. 39)

(27 Sept 10) Monday: I received a very significant phone call from my new bank, informing me of their approval of my new and increased equity line of credit; AMEN! There's that "HOLY

SPIRIT PRAYER POWER" coming to the rescue again (CPA) I discovered additional good news as follows: This generates Pearl no. 53, but it is also the 16th pearl this month which breaks the monthly HOLY SPIRIT intervention record, so far; additionally, it becomes my second "TRIPLE-WHAMMY" of 3 concentric circles around "27"; after the translation process occurs 2010 to 2007 as usual; here are the three post-evidentiary effects involved; 1) My reconciliation with my brother William before his "Passing On"; 2) Jim Rost near-death experience in Iraq, his link to my near-death experience (same year 2007) 3) This equity line approval (3 circles). THANK YOU HEAVENLY FATHER! We do have an "AWESOME GOD", as I have reiterated many times in this journal; to emphasize his almighty power.

183. Student Visa Extension Of Two Years For Martine (NCIC, Rebecca) (CPA no. 40)

(30 Sept 10) Thursday: No. 54 Pearl occurs today when I received a phone call this evening from my new (NCIC), meaning; NEW CREATURE IN CHRIST (see effect no. 36 and 71) Martine who now becomes, thanks to the HOLY SPIRIT intervention in her life; one of my best friends, along with her (17 year old) daughter ANNE; we're like father and daughter's now; getting back to the good news the call generated was: A definite novena prayer was answered (CPA) when Martine told me her student VISA was being extended for 2 years; I had been adding this petition to my list after I met her (recall the same day 03 May 10 I met Nina, and she asked me to pray, "that she could stay in this country"; VIOLA! GOD answered in only 4 months; my readers can see that these Pearls, points or solutions to miracle equation (Yl=70) and also its associated "STRING OF PEARLS"; are accumulating rapidly on their journey to infinity (eternity in Heaven; as the analogy portrays) in my earlier explanation the meaning of these post-evidentiary effects; so let's continue with the additional Pearls; THIS SAME DAY pearl no. 55 is produced, when "my special Angel"; Nina introduces me to her Filipino friend (also a Catholic who believes in miracles) Rebecca; a potential (NCIC); my being led to her as always by "GOD'S HOLY SPIRIT"; after my usual MODUS OPERANDI, meaning method of operation, informing

NEW, "children of GOD"; I am drawn to; she requested a copy of no. 611 miracle bible since this would be her first bible ever in her life; I said I would purchase one for her next week; she was very happy and she now becomes another, (as it were) daughter of mine; THANKS AGAIN FATHER! For your continued blessings on this journey through time; designed by you of course; you being the engineer; this time; not me; although you gave me my talent as an engineer for 30 years; beginning with my graduation in 1962.

184.　　Recalling My Apostolic Mission From My Near-Death Experience

(02 Oct 10) Saturday: I need to digress at this point for the generation of an "All Important Pearl no. 56" I mentioned previously, (see effect no. 1A) that "GOD'S HOLY SPIRIT" wasn't through me yet; the proof being my passing through this merit phase I'm in; involving my future life and transformation to an (NCIC), as above. I paid my debt to my Heavenly Father when my apostolic mission directed by him was established instantly, during my encounter with "The Dome Of Creation", by rewarding me for my conversion with (so far) a total of 56 pearls in only 45 months, recall that GOD says in HIS word, "there will be joy among the Angels of GOD over ONE sinner who repents, moreover ninety nine who have no need of repentance"; that one sinner was definitely me; also, this date (02 Oct 10) after translation from 2010 to 2007 falls on a Tuesday, meaning, it becomes another math coordinate in the so called "PLANE OF PEARLS" containing the miracle equation $(Y1=70)$; the plane is defined by three points or values, $(y,0,x)$ where $y=Y3=74$ years of my life 2011 (so far); 0" the origin or simply my date of birth (22 May 37) and finally x= infinity or ETERNITY WITH GOD IN HEAVEN our ultimate goal as an analogy, remember, this plane and $(Y1=70)$ miracle equation, is approaching infinity as its limit while its height (years of my life) is increasing until I "PASS ON" to my HEAVENLY FATHER.

185.　　Meeting no. 2 With Edwin (Deliverance From Alcohol)

(23 Oct 10) Saturday: Last evening I received probably, "the most important phone call since this journey began"; Edwin called,

(see effect no. 181) recall that I met him at Nativity park near the statue of, "Our Lady Of Fatima" (25 Sept 10); he was very upset and probably would have harmed himself if the "HOLY SPIRIT" hadn't led me to him; he verified this fact during our first meeting when I revealed my near-death experience to him; I was surprised but delighted when he said, "me and the HOLY SPIRIT has changed his life forever" he is a new creature (NCIC) in only ONE month's time and proved it to me on this date a Saturday; as before; we both attended 5 p.m. mass and received communion; I could see the transformation of Edwin into that new creature as we all would like to experience GOD'S power in our lives; he had a glow about him that I will never forget; a wonderful sign of happiness, peace and contentment; he is on the "String Of Pearls", for this date (23 Oct 10) falls on a Tuesday, when translated back from 2010 to 2007; and becomes Pearl no. 57 on the solution to the miracle equation, as always, (Yl=70) I left him with miracle bible no. 611 and a copy of an update of my MOM'S prayer (see effect no. 9); we parted with big smiles and I told him to use GOD'S tools that he now has in his possession; also told him to do whatever his caretakers and sponsor recommends; he assured me he would; so far, this is a great success narrative.

186. Yemen Al-Qaeda And "Washington Connection" Bomb Plots Thwarted (WPA no. 57 and no. 58)

(30 Oct 10) Saturday: Today a Yemeni student and her mother were arrested by Yemen authorities and charged with conspiracy to bomb cargo planes on flights to the U.S.; this I call, the "Yemen Connections"; this week there was the Washington connection"; similar to the popular movie, "The French Connection"; but in lieu of drugs involved, it is now BOMBS; in the aforementioned Washington case; a man was arrested for trying to kill some of MY neighbors, who use the metro transit system to commute to D.C. everyday; this psychopath was ready to plant bombs on the metro-trains and kill thousands of people simultaneously; but thanks to the FBI and subsequently "HOLY SPIRIT PRAYER POWER", which I have been using since my NDE (09 Jan 07); GOD answered my (57th and 58th WPA, combined plot types); THANKS LORD! These are two good examples of pure hate and

evil we face in today's world; definitely a product of "Satan's Rath" and further demonstrating his ownership of our world; recall GOD'S words: "I am leaving, for the ruler of the world is coming (referring to Satan, the devil) but he has no power over me; I will send you, the advocate; (THE HOLY SPIRIT) to be your guide and protector from all temptation and evil to come"; (paraphrased); additionally, I learned in "Natural Theology" (knowing GOD through nature); Satan is the author of all evil; while GOD is the author of all good; but must permit the existence of evil, because it is one of the imperfections of nature; GOD is the only perfection or non-contingent being; meaning, he is necessary for all existence; by definition HE is FIRST (FUNDAMENTAL); everything in the universe; including and especially man, IS CONTINGENT; meaning "it didn't have to be", everything relies on another for its existence; this can be easily proven through cause and effect principles from deductive reasoning used by philosophy; in this case, "the Philosophy of GOD"; by definition; philosophy isn't SIMPLY ONE'S OPINION; but it is, "the science of the ultimate causes of ALL things as known by reason"; meaning, it deals with things in their first cause; it is fundamentally based on a search for the truth through logical reasoning; besides there can only be "ONE truth not many"; BECAUSE TRUTH IS SINGULAR; and recall in the preface that the test of truth is the objective evidence since GOD is first and necessary, HE is known (and can be proven to be as mentioned above) as the, "UNCAUSED CAUSE" (see effect no. 42); meaning, nothing caused HIM, HE caused himself HE was always in existence; this date (30 Oct 10) not only generates the 58th Pearl but as mentioned above also the 57th and 58th WPA the latter referring to the, "war on terror" using the translation process, as always; from 2010 back to 2007; this date falls on a Tuesday on my miracle calendar (see graphics effect no. 30) for (R=58) and (N=365 math calculation of the number of combinations possible with days in 2007) estimated to be 10^{116}; once again demonstrating GOD'S unique and awesome power as this function approaches infinity (or eternity) rapidly; explained in the, "Plane of the Pearls." I included here more math proof because it is fascinating to reveal this aspect of "HOLY SPIRIT POWER."

187.   Connie's Miracle On "All Saint Day" Revealed

(01 Nov l0) "All Saints Day" Monday: While doing my customary shopping at Wal-Mart after attending daily mass; I literally (being led by the spirit) ran into CONNIE while recalling that today is Nina's; "my Special Angels" 51st birthday (I'll explain later); I was looking in the men's section for items and she was the employee answering my questions; the spirit led me to ask, "if she believed in miracles"; to which she replied, "of course, doesn't everyone?"; then she told me about her brother, who had been rushed to the emergency room, because he was bleeding from his colon; his briefs were soaked with blood; she was frantic, as were all of her family; they were extremely worried; the surgeon found NO apparent cause for his severe condition; he was NORMAL and IN NO PAIN; the doctors had no sufficient explanation and he left the hospital after an "overnight" observation in perfect health; as if the crisis never occurred in the first place; Connie and her family and the doctors knew they witnessed, "A Miracle"; recall: Father Pio before his passing had exhibited the bleeding of the, "five wounds of CHRIST', on his body for years; that was true not simply folklore; so the family went to visit his shrine to thank him and no other incident has happened since; her brother is normal; they all rejoiced; this certainly constitutes Pearl no. 60, because Nina's birthday takes Pearl no. 59; her birthday is ahead of my meeting with Connie, since my mind was focused on Nina exclusively that morning; so there it is (2 significant events); another "DOUBLE WHAMMY" by the HOLY SPIRIT for this special day' two concentric circles around (01 Nov 07) Thursday due to the date translation of 2010 back to 2007; THANK YOU HEAVENLY FATHER for all the merit given to me in this fantastic venture spanning now, 46 months, In passing; 60 pearls would make (R=60) and to emphasize once again our creators power demo. (10^{120}) is reached. TALK ABOUT REJOICING. WOW! I was aiming to end this journal at this 187th post-evidentiary investigation, but I must continue on because additional gifts or pearls are forth coming from a Holy Spirit Prompt I received on this important day.

188.   Drug Cartel Leader Killed (CPA no. 41)

(06 Nov 10) Saturday: It should be noted at this time on (04 Nov 10) I realized not only is 60 total pearls apparent, but today also coincides with the end of my 60th novena (9 days of prayer each) yielding (60x9) or a total of 540 days of prayer since my near death experience, additionally on this same day (06 Nov 10) Tony Tormenta a notorious drug cartel leader is killed. Pearl 61 and CPA 41 occurs because this date falls on a Tuesday 07. Thank you Lord! Again answering my morning prayers. Today lies in "The Plane of the Pearls."

189.   Martine Reports a "Joy Shot from the Spirit"

(08 Nov 10) Monday: My special angel Martine called me on this pearl 62 day translating back to 2007 falls on a Thursday and reported a "what I call", joy shot from the HOLY SPIRIT due to her continuing NCIC status; we both were elated and pleased today.

190.   Zahra Baker (Rest In Glory) RIG (CPA no. 42) British Couple Released (CPA no. 43)

(13 Nov 10) Saturday: Pearl 63 and 64, CPA 42 and 43 occurred today when two events happen. First a young North Carolina girls body (Zahra Baker) was found and second a British couple who had been held hostage for months, were released by the Somali pirates unharmed. Thank you father for answering two prayers in one day. The translation process brings this date to Tuesday in 2007.

191.   Girl Kidnapped Found Alive (CPA no. 44)

(15 Nov 10) Monday: A missing 13 year old girl was found alive in Ohio when her kidnapper Hoffan was arrested after he had murdered her parents in Virginia and taken her with him to Ohio. Thanks father for saving this poor girl. Pearl 65 and CPA 44 in translation falls on a Thursday 2007.

192.   Met Nina's children From Maryland

(27 Nov 10) Saturday: On this pearl 66 day I met Felicia (see effect No. 171) and Nina's other wonderful children, besides Felicia for the very first time of our 7 months relationship and I was thoroughly impressed by their intelligence; their father had done an excellent job of raising them (Delina, Sharita and a boy Jameel) all attending universities in Maryland another daughter (Saturnina) is in Germany studying to be a doctor of Psychiatry and in her 4th year. This date falls on a Tuesday in 2007; thus a pearl is gifted.

193.   Drug Dealer in Mexico Arrested (CPA no. 45)

(29 Nov 10) Monday: Today both Edwin (the cured alcoholic in just 1 month) and Martine (NCIC's) reported joy shots from the Holy Spirit pearl 67 and 68, CPA 45. Criminal to justice prayer answered when a small victory over drugs in Mexico occurred when a drug dealer, who killed 30 people, was arrested. This date falls on a Thursday in 2007 (2 gifted pearls from the Holy Spirit), Thanks Lord!

194.   Al-Qaeda False Documents Criminal Enterprise Busted (WPA no. 59)

(02 Dec 10) Thursday: A criminal enterprise was busted today that made false identification documents for Al Qaeda; pearl 69 is generated along with WPA 59, a war prayer answered. This happens to be a significant event eligible for "the plane of the Pearls" only; because it doesn't fall on a Tuesday or a Thursday in 2007 which would have been directly on the string of pearls (Y1=70).

195.   Seven Months Anniversary Reminder of my "Special Angels"

(03 Dec 10) Friday: This date marks seven months (Remember no. 7 means, "totality of perfection") (see effect no. 37) since I was led by the spirit to Nina, Martine and her daughter Anne; thus Pearl 70 is realized in "the plane of the pearls."

196. Ronni Chasen's Killer Commits Suicide (CPA no. 46)

(04 Dec 10) Saturday: Pearl 71 and CPA 46 occurs today when a man named Smith commits suicide after police learn, he was responsible for the death of a Hollywood celebrity (Ronni Chasen) found in her car in an apparent accident; later it was established an attempted robbery and carjacking was the cause. Thanks Lord! For answering quickly my criminal to justice prayer; I had added this to my pray list; translation process lands this date on a Tuesday in 2007 and therefore directly on the string of pearls equation (Y1=70).

197. Julian Assange Arrested for Rape (CPA no. 47)

(06 Dec 10) Monday: Wikki leaks founder (Julian Assange) was arrested and jailed for rape in Sweden. This constitutes pearl 72 and CPA 47 translation of this date to 2007 falls on a Thursday. Thanks to Holy Spirit prayer power this criminal, who was leaking classified documents online, is off the street temporarily because he has his supporters and they will do their best to exonerate him; but creator God will thwart their attempts.

198. Kidnapped Girl Found Unharmed Abductor Arrested (CPA no. 48)

(11 Dec 10) Saturday: A missing 12 year old girl and her abductor, who earlier murdered her mother in Virginia was found in North Carolina; thus pearl 73 and CPA 48 is gifted by the Holy Spirit. Thanks Father! For preventing another murder. Translation process lands on a Tuesday and directly on string equation (Y1=70).

199. Young People Believe My NDE

(13 Dec 10) Monday: Two High School student (brothers) visiting Virginia from Hawaii one of them named Junior believes in the Dome miracles; unusual for teenagers these days; Pearl 74 is generated today because this date after using translation process falls on a Thursday in 2007 squarely on the string equation (Y1=70).

200.   Six Pearls Gifted in One Day Also (CPA no. 49)

(20 Dec 10) Monday: Today something very unusual happened with the Holy Spirit sending me, for the very first time, a one day total of six pearls which is equivalent to "6" concentric circles around (20 Dec 07) Thursday due to the date translation of 2010 back to 2007; thanks heavenly Father! For your outstanding continuing blessing bestowed on me, your servant, in this modern world today; I understand fully your awesome power demonstration at this juncture. The pearls under discussion here are as follows: Pearl 75 and CPA 49= a civilian prayer answered due to my reminding you, my readers, that "we need signs from the Holy Spirit, to enhance our faith in him in these troubling times."

2) My favorite Uncle Vic (Victor Christy) was buried today; yielding pearl 76.

3) Monday in Rosary Parlance for Catholics, means, "The joyful mysteries" are used pearl 77.

4) Martine reported to me a joy shot from the Holy Spirit at (2:40 A.M.) this morning pearl 78.

5) Nina's first visit to the unemployment office (VEC) was a success because she qualified for funds, Pearl 79.

6) Edwin called and said, "he has been a counselor for men in his "Alcoholics anonymous" meetings (see effect no. 181) For his amazing transformation to an (NCIC) in only one month after being touched by the Holy Spirit, pearl 80.

Note: All of the above pearls leads to an equation given me by Spirit Prompt, as follows: (see effect no. 37) "Totality of perfection= 7= TDPL (NDE) Where T= Time of Pearl (clock time) D= Date of Pearl

L= Link and NDE= My Near-Death Experience. If one counts the number of characters in this equation the total is (7) as indicated VOILA! Isn't the Holy Spirit Mysterious?

201.   Benazir Bhutto Justice (WPA no. 60)

Weapons Trafficking Via Iran, Man Arrested (WPA no. 61)
(22 Dec 10) Wednesday: Two police officials are arrested in the Benazir Bhutto (RIG), assassination in Pakistan (see effect no. 94) this yields pearl 81 and WPA 60-61= a man seized in Kandahar,, Afghanistan today tied to weapon's trafficking Via Iran. Thanks

Lord! For bringing some long awaited justice for a wonderful soul in Heaven (Benazir Bhutto) as well as preventing weapons from reaching our enemies. This date considered because these were certainly significant events landing in "The plane of the Pearls" translating back to 2007.

202. Jesus Christmas Story Matches Journal Symbol

(25 Dec 10) Saturday (Christmas Day): Today during my celebration of the birth of Christ I discovered in my church bulletin after mass, a perfect match for "J" standing for Jesus story and my symbol for this journal consisting of a "J" also, at the center of a surrounding circle. Pearl 82 thank you baby Jesus! For gifting me this pearl on this glorious day because this date falls exactly on Tuesday 2007 after using the now familiar translation process from 2010.

203. Reconciliation with Nina's Tenants

(27 Dec 10) Monday: Today my reconciliation with all residents at Nina's House after some testy words were exchanged was evident; I recalled that my father in heaven says, "we must forgive others their trespasses if we want ours forgiven" (The Most Familiar prayer from HIS word," the Our Father.") Thus Pearl 83 was added today to my repertoire; translating this date from 2010 back to 2007 falls on a Thursday; thanks Holy Spirit for giving me empathy for my new friends without animosity.

204. Led by the Spirit to Kim

(29 Dec 10) Wednesday: A significant event occurred today when I was led by the spirit to a woman at Nativity Church named Kim; it turns out that after telling her about my Near Death experience of 2007, she just happened to be a graphic designer, whom I thought would be perfect to do the graphic illustrating required for my journal; but to my dismay she told me she was busy on a project for "The blessed Virgin Mary", so I backed off because "Our Mother Mary" is more important"; she loved my NDE explanation and assured me prayerfully, that the HOLY SPIRIT would solve my problem (by the way she was correct) I did find the solution because it takes patience. The solution was simple,

after some serious reflection on my part, I used my engineering drawing skills to do the project myself; and it turned out great. Thus Pearl 84 is born an addition to the "Plane of the Pearls" since the event is significant as mentioned above and directly links to my NDE; my gratitude to my father in Heaven for leading me to my engineering degree.

205.   Shelly's Recovery From Stroke (CPA no. 50)

(04 Jan 11) Tuesday: My friend Shelly who suffered a stroke and I prayed earnestly for her, returned to daily mass today; as she hadn't attended mass for a long time; but somewhat handicapped by her post-stroke condition now; my prayer of course was answered Pearl 85 and CPA 50 comes into being; Thanks to Holy Spirit prayer power! For the translation date back to 2007 falls on a Thursday meeting the criteria for Pearl generation and linking directly to my NDE; because she was at the pinnacle of my prayer list since we loved her so much.

206.   First American Saint John Neuman Celebration

(05 Jan 11) Wednesday: Today we celebrated "The Feast of our First American Saint John Neuman"; thus the Holy Spirit's gift is pearl 86 because this date after translation back to 2007 lies in "The Plane of the Pearls" and he was a Bishop and a Cardinal from Pennsylvania right next to my hometown in Ohio, before being recently canonized a Saint.

207.   President Karsi and Vice President Afghanistan Attacks Thwarted (WPA no. 62)

(06 Jan 11) Thursday: Pearl 87 and WPA 62 occurred today when a war prayer answered to qualify for the main significant event as follows: Afghan officials thwarted two major attacks:

1.   Five would be homicide bombers were arrested during an attempt to kill the Vice President of Afghanistan.
2.   A bomb near President Karsi's palace was discovered and detonated safely to save his life.

This date after transposition 2010 back to 2007 would lie in "The Plane of the Pearls not coinciding with the string equation Y1=70."

208. Fourth Anniversary of my NDE "Baptism of the Lord" Celebration

(09 Jan 11) Sunday: Today two definite significant events occur since we celebrate "The Baptism of the Lord" and also my 4th anniversary of my NDE (09 Jan 07) this is a pearl 88 and 89 day because translation back to 2007 lands on a Tuesday exactly on the miracle equation (Y1=70).

209. Gifford Recovery from Attempted Assassination (CPA no. 51)

(11 Jan 11) Tuesday: I had added Representative Gifford (who was almost assassinated by a psychopathic personality killer in Arizona last week to the top of my morning prayer list and thanks to a pearl 90 and CPA 51 my prayer has been answered and she is recovering; breathing on her own. Thank you Holy Spirit! For stepping up to the plate and keeping such a wonderful soul with us; this date through translation to 2007 falls on a Thursday. AMEN!

210. Al Anwar Alwaki Sentenced in Absentia (WPA no. 63)

(16 Jan 11) Sunday: Pearl 91 and WPA 63 breaks into the top spot today when a Yemeni court sentences a radical cleric (Al-Anwar Alwaki) formerly in America, in absentia; at least now we are getting closer to bringing him to justice; (see effect no. 100) for our first unsuccessful crack at him. This date of course is a genuine pearl since its translation to 2007 lands on a Tuesday; remember reader, that the math coordinate is the pearl in question especially if falls on a Tuesday or Thursday of the month in 2007; the year of my Near-Death Experience.

211. Cocaine Bust in Spain and Sex Trafficking Crime Family Convicted (CPA no. 52)

(18 Jan 11) Tuesday: A very special day in my life today; my son Donald's 47th birthday. In terms of our discussion here in regards

to Pearls From the Holy Spirit one CPA, no. 52; criminals brought to justice are as follows for Pearl 92:

1. A Romanian sex trafficking crime family was convicted today in the U.K.
2. The largest ever sophisticated cocaine bust in Spain linked to the Zeta cartel in Mexico with the capture of a notorious drug leader.

Again our translation process yields the above mentioned pearl; because this date coincides with Thursday in 2007.

212.   Gambino Crime Family Leader Arrested (CPA no. 53)

(20 Jan 11) Thursday: The FBI today arrested the Mafia Chief (Gambino) and 120 total Colombo Crime Family members for extortion; murder and Narcotic's trafficking; certainly this qualifies for pearl 93 and CPA 53. Thanks Holy Spirit! For eliminating these dangerous long-time criminals from the streets of our larger cities and outside these United States; this was a very significant catch; the pearl lies in "The Plane of the Pearls" with the miracle equation Y1=70.

213.   Representative Gifford to Rehab (CPA no. 54)

(21 Jan 11) Friday: In just 13 days a "Living Miracle" occurred; representative Gifford was transferred to a rehab memorial hospital in Houston, Texas where she is recovering nicely from a devastating attempt on her life; Pearl 94 and CPA 54 is realized today. Thanks Father! For answering my and others fervent prayers for one your best Senatorial children.

214.   Edwin's Alcoholic Problem Still Under Control (NCIC)

(23 Jan 11) Sunday: Edwin called this morning (my former alcoholic NCIC) and said "He is still counseling AA members while avoiding alcohol use in his life"; he is "letting the spirit lead him now and praying often, taking my original advice since I was led to him at "Our Lady of Fatima Statue" in Nativity Park adjacent to the church parking area (25 Sept 10) (see effect no. 181); I know he will never relapse because he had a special conversion from the Holy Spirit's Power, Pearl 95. It can happen to all of us when

God looks at our goodness and rewards us because he loves HIS children so much; Edwin is selected for his outstanding work in avoiding the evil's of alcohol and returning to his heavenly father. Today after translation process lands on Tuesday 2007.

215.   Fourth Anniversary of Miracle Calendar Linear Relationship "Conversion of St. Paul" Celebration

(25 Jan 11) Tuesday: Pearl 96 is born today because not only does it coincide with a Thursday in 2007, but this is my 4th anniversary of my miracle calendar discovery of linear function links to my near-death experience; also it is the celebrated reminder of "The Conversion of St. Paul" when he encountered the Lord on his way to Damascus as a converted man named Saul.

216.   Test for Dog Casey's Possible Cancer Negative (CPA no. 55)

(01 Feb 11) Tuesday: I have been thinking of my brother Fabian's dog Casey today since he called me (31 Jan 11) to request using my prayer list for Casey's possible skin cancer; Pearl 97 and CPA 55 was the answer from the Holy Spirit today; all tests are negative but he does need a pathological study to determine what stage he is in: one through four are possible diagnosis. Further prayer is needed, for Casey is not "out" of the woods yet. I am still actively praying for a favorable outcome since this would be his 4th healing. This pearl is genuine and coincides with Thursday 2007.

217.   Pat Healed of Kidney Disease (CPA no. 56)

(06 Feb 11) Sun: Martine requested my prayers to the Holy Spirit for her bosses father Pat's healing of his kidney disease (04 Feb 11). Pearl 98 and CPA 56 was an immediate spirit answer; as he says in HIS word "if you ask for anything in my name I will give it to you"; HE complied completely and absolutely! Today Pat was healed. After transposing this date to 2007 it lands on Thursday. Thanks Holy Spirit for Pat's healing!

218. Led by Spirit to Woman Named Happy ("Dome of Sky" Reading)

(07 Feb 11) Monday: An unexpected significant event occurred today, when I was led to an oriental woman named Happy; she had attended 7:30 a.m. mass daily, but this day of our meeting was planned because after relating my NDE to her and her believing the Dome and the resulting miracles; the reading today was "the Dome of the Sky in Genesis" sound familiar? (see effect no. 3) Happy gave me a prayer request for a job for her son Joseph, who has an MBA degree but was unable to find work in his field of study in these difficult times; I believe the spirit will answer soon. Pearl 99 is the signature of that assurance because today lies in the all-important "Plane of the Pearls" after transition to 2007.

219. "Our Lady of Lourdes" and "World Day of Sick"

(11 Feb 11) Friday: Pearl 100 and 101 come forward today from the spirit with the celebration of "Our Lady of Lourdes" feast day coinciding with "World Day of the Sick" and another call from my best direct evidence NCIC person' Edwin, he says "He is fine and has "turned the corner" in his new life; that certainly qualifies two pearls of which both lie in "The Plane of the Pearls" heading back to 2007.

220. Final Positive Report for Dog Casey's Prognosis (CPA no. 57)

(15 Feb 11) Tuesday: My brother Fabian called today to give me some wonderful news about Casey's results of his final pathological reports the stage of his cancer is in fact stage no. 1; meaning, his dog is completely cleared of cancer. Holy Spirit prayer power has healed Casey for the 4th time to alleviate all fears. Thanks again father for keeping him with his family who love him dearly. Pearl 102 and CPA 57 is gifted today and falls on Thursday, after the translation process to 2007.

221. Judy's Successful Transformation and Conversion (CPA no. 58)

(22 Feb 11) Tuesday: I called Judy today after not hearing from her for months; my prayers for her were answered when she informed me she no longer needed crutches anymore and had lost

a significant amount of weight on her way to a life without her beloved son Patrick whom she finally buried in Pennsylvania; (see effect no. 49) my petitions to the spirit for her conversion began (May 2010) which shows we must have patience and perseverance in our prayer life for this type of outcome rejoicing for Pearl 103 and CPA 58 for Judy. I'm looking forward to our next meeting to see for myself her transformation as another NCIC. Today after transition to 2007 falls exactly on Thursday. Thank you Holy Spirit! For recognizing Judy's remarkable strength and all important love for you; you rewarded her.

222. First Copy of Print Out of Journal

(27 Feb 11) Sunday: I gave the very first copy of my printed journal to Father Wilson with his blessing; a day where a wonderful baseball player "passes on" (Duke Snider, formerly with the Brooklyn Dodgers) (RIG) Duke; this was certainly a significant pearl 104 considering these two events happening on the same day. The transition to 2007 of course falling on Tuesday.

223. Message no. 27 (SPIRIT PROMPT) Pearls Are Blue and Match Virgin Mary's Sash and Dome Sky (CPA no. 59)

(01 Mar 11) Tuesday: Martine told me that her daughter who had scored 1900 points on her SAT test out of a possible 2400, was offered a $13,000 scholarship from a Virginia College; additionally, I received my 27th message this morning in the usual middle of the night as follows: "the Pearls I have given you are blue matching the sky in the Dome and the sash of the blessed virgin Mary" (see effect no. 30 and 31) Pearl 105 and CPA 59 are resulting prayer answer from the Holy Spirit and due to transition to 2007 lands squarely on Thursday.

224. I Received Copyrights for Journal (CPA no. 60)

(04 Mar 11) Friday: Pearl 106 and CPA 60. Arrive from the spirit since my copyrights were approved today for my journal and therefore lie in "The Plane of the Pearls"; another significant prayer answer from God.

225.   Failed Hijacking of Flight from Paris to Rome (CPA no. 61)

(24 Apr 11) Easter Sunday: Pearl 107 and CPA 61. A failed hijacking of a Alitalia flight from Paris to Rome; a man put a nail clipper file to the throat of a female flight attendant demanding the plane be flown to the Libyan Capital of Tripoli; crew and passengers overpowered the man and he was arrested when the plane landed in Rome. Police identified him as a 48 years old citizen of Kazakhstan who worked in Paris. The flight attendant was treated for minor injuries no one else was hurt. Thank you Father for answering one of my morning prayers for bringing all criminals to justice, especially on this very special day, your resurrection from the dead to save us for eternal life with you in heaven. This special date lies squarely on a Tuesday in 2007.

226.   Al Qaeda Senior Leader Killed (WPA no. 64)

(26 Apr 11) Tuesday: Abu Hafsal-Najdia senior leader of Al-Qaeda in Afghanistan. Pearl 108 and WPA 64 thanks Lord! One of the big boys eliminated. This date after translation to 2007 falls on Thursday.

227.   Michael Douglas Cleared of Cancer (CPA no. 62) Also Crystal Beth (CPA no. 63)

(27 Apr 11) Wednesday: Pearl 109 and CPA 62 and 63. Michael Douglas announces his throat cancer is cleared. An answer to my morning prayers thanks to Holy Spirit prayer power, additionally my friend Joe told me on 07 Jan 11 to pray for his daughter Crystal Beth who was having at that time a test of a mass that was present on her ovaries. On this date we can all rejoice for Crystal Beth's test for cancer was cleared according to Joe.

228.   Osama Bin Laden Killed (WPA no. 65) and (CPA no. 64)

(01 May 11) Sunday: Divine mercy Sunday Pearls 110-115 (six pearls today) as follows:

1.   Divine Mercy Sunday 2) Mass for beatification of John Paul II 3) Dad's watch linked to my NDE. 4) Donna's link to my NDE. 5) Date (09 Jan 07): Tues 2007 Pearl. 6) Osama Bin Laden killed in Pakistan compound. A big big

thank you Holy Spirit! CPA 64 morning prayer answered and WPA 65 novena prayer answered.

229. Abu Sayyaf Al Qaeda Extremist Arrested (WPA no. 66)

(08 May 11) Sunday (Mother's Day): Pearl 116 and WPA 66 police in the Philippines say they've captured a militant with an Al-Qaeda linked movement in an operation at a manila shopping center. Police arrested Asdatul Sahirun at a shopping in the capital's malate tourist district; he is a suspected member of Abu Sayyaf extremist movement. Thank you Holy Spirit for answering another of my morning prayers on a very special day of my 2nd life. Happy Mother's Day to all of my mom readers and of course, my blessed mother in Heaven and my earthly mom who is also there in Heaven since the 17th of January 87. After translation to 2007 this date lands on a Tuesday.

230. Terrorists Arrested in Attempted Bombing New York City (CPA no. 65) and (WPA no. 67)

(13 May 11) Friday: Pearl 117 and CPA 65, WPA 67. "Our Lady of Fatima" remembrance supposed to be an unlucky day Friday the 13th, but today (2) would be terrorists were arrested in New York City. They wanted to blow-up the Empire State building; (2) psychopaths (lone-wolves) and also to destroy synagogues and kill Jews. A WPA 67 for God; a CPA 65 is realized today; a prayer answer for a man with AK-47 attempted to enter a military base in Maryland and chases by M.P.'s with police in pursuit also; the man was shooting from a stolen vehicle during the chase; thank God that he was caught on the Missouri campus where classes were not in session. A big thank you for Holy Spirit prayer power and police intervention. This date lies in "The Plane of the Pearls" after transition to 2007.

231. Drug Gang Leader Arrested in Mexico (CPA no. 66 and 67) and (WPA no. 68) Hafiz Khan Arrested

(14 May 11) Saturday: Pearl 118, CPA 66 and 67. Mexican authorities capture a top leader of the Sinaloa Drug Gang. Thank you Holy Spirit for answering my morning prayers for bringing

this criminal to justice for the Mexican people; also a child trafficking ring leader busted in China, another answer to my morning prayers.WPA 68=Federal authorities arrested a Miami imam and two of his son's on charges they provided $50,000 to the Pakistani Taliban (Hafiz Muhammed Sher Ali Khan). One son was arrested in Margate, Florida while the other was detained in Los Angeles, all three men are U.S. Citizens. Hafiz Khan's daughter, grandson and another unrelated man are also named in the indictment and remain at large in Pakistan. Thanks Holy Spirit for bringing child traffickers especially to criminal justice, a most despicable crime in our society today. This date lies in "The Plane of the Pearls" after transition to 2007.

232.   Al Qaeda Operative in Yemen Arrested (WPA no. 69)

(17 May 11) Tuesday: Pearl 119 and WPA 69. A Senior Al-Qaeda operative in Yemen was arrested in Karachi, Pakistan. The man who uses the Alias (Abu Sohaib Al-Makki) is a Yemen national; Pakistan Army says "the man had been working directly under Al-Qaeda leaders along the border with Afghanistan." Thanks father for answering my morning prayer! You captured one "big fish."

233.   Mexican Army Finds Migrants Alive (CPA no. 68 and 69)

(18 May 11) Wednesday: Pearl 120 and CPA 68 and 69. Mexican authorities have found 513 migrants jammed in (2) U.S. trucks; the largest find in recent years. Thanks father for rescuing your children from this evil! Note: This is the "Feast of St. John (the Pope)" in the Catholic Church today; "Pope John"; additionally, my prayer for Father Martin, who was ill has been answered today at Nativity Church; he said the 7:30 mass this morning looking very healthy again; thanks again Holy Spirit for answering my 212th prayer since my NDE in 2007. This is "The Plane of the Pearls" date in 2007.

234.   Journalist Dorothy Parvaz Released Unharmed (CPA no. 70)

(19 May 11) Thursday: Pearl 121 and CPA 70 (Sig. Event) Dorothy Parvaz an Al Jazzera journalist kidnapped (29 Apr 11) has been released, unharmed and is back in Doha. Thank you Lord for

answering my morning prayer for her safe return to those who love and miss her; many prayers were uplinked to you and you sent that all important downlink; also Happy 44th birthday to my "special angel" Martine who the Holy Spirit led me to (03 May 10) a very special soul in my now 2nd life. Today also lies in "The Plane of the Pearls" in 2007.

235.   Martine's Uncle Recovers from Stroke (CPA no. 71)

(20 May 11) Friday: Pearl 122 and CPA 71. Martine called and said her Uncle Anthony is talking and has fully recovered from his stroke; prayer answered; thanks heavenly father! Today of course lies in "The Plane of the Pearls" transferred to 2007.

236.   Drug Cartel Leader of "The Gulf" Arrested (CPA no. 72)

(21 May 11) Sat: Pearl 123 and CPA 72 the Mexican government has arrested a leader of the Gulf Drug Cartel; thank you Lord for this answer to my morning prayers; we'll get them all eventually. "Plane of the Pearls" date in 2007.

237.   Top Al Qaeda Leader Arrested in Uzbekistan (WPA no. 70)

(20 Apr 11) Wednesday (out of seq.): Pearl 124 and WPA 70. Two significant events occurred today when a top Al-Qaeda leader was arrested in Uzbekistan and two other terrorists captured by NATO forces in Afghanistan. Thanks Lord for these "Plane of the Pearls" incidents translated back to 2007.

238.   Mob Boss of Philadelphia, Pennsylvania Arrested (CPA no. 73)

(24 May 11) Tuesday: Pearl 125 and CPA 73 Feds arrested reputed Philly mob boss Joseph "Uncle Joe" Ligambi and 12 others; the men face charges including conspiracy, extortion, illegal gambling and witness tampering; Ligambi was sentenced to life in prison in 1989 for a 1985 killing, but the conviction was overturned and he was released in 1997. Thanks Holy Spirit for answering another criminal to justice prayer. Today coincides with (Y1=70).

239.   Found Publisher for my Journal (CPA no. 74)

(27 May 11) Friday: Pearl 126 and CPA 74 PROMPT FROM SPIRIT: To contact Christian bookstore in Springfield Plaza leads me to my publisher for this journal; Thomas Nelson publishers in Tennessee. Referred me to their affiliate Westbow Press in Indiana well known publishers for Christian Books. The final design will be (6"x9") size with other design characteristics to be negotiated later; thanks Holy Spirit for answering my fervent prayer! "Plane of the Pearls" date in 2007.

240.   Ratko Mladic Arrested for Genocide and other War Crimes (WPA no. 71)

(29 May 11) Sunday: Pearl 127 and WPA 71. Former Army Chief General Ratko Mladic is indicted for atrocities committed during the Serbian 1992-1995 war. Basically genocide and war crimes against 8,000 innocent unarmed citizens. Thanks Lord! He must be punished in the Hague Tribune because he was the commander of the Bosnian-Serbian Army during this time period. Today falls on Tuesday in 2007 directly on Y1=70.

241.   Terrorist Arrested in France (WPA no. 72)

(30 May 11) Memorial Day Monday: Pearl 128 and WPA 72 French prosecutor opens a preliminary investigation for murder and attempted murder in connection with the April 28 terror bombing in Marrakech, Morocco. France is investigating because eight French tourists were among the 17 killed when the blast tore through the Argana Café in Marrakech's old town district; authorities have arrested six in the case including one with suspected ties to Al-Qaeda. Thanks Holy Spirit for this war prayer answer! One day at a time, one war criminal at a time to justice. "Plane of the Pearls" date in 2007.

242.   Anne Will Do the Re-typing of the Journal (CPA no. 75)

(31 May 11) Tuesday: Pearl 129 and CPA 75. Today on the feast of the visitation of the B.V.M my prayer was answered because Martine said "Anne will be able to transfer the re-typing of the journal to a computer disc", so I can send the disc to my publisher

Westbow Press. I was petitioning the Holy Spirit for this to happen since I didn't have access to the original computer. Thanks heavenly Father! For answering quickly. Today coincides exactly with the string equation (Y1=70) after translating to 2007.

243.   Cocaine Seized in Paraguay (WPA no. 73)

(01 Jun 11) Wednesday: Pearl 130 and WPA 73. Authorities in Paraguay seize more than 1,900 pounds of Cocaine disguised as bags of rice; official say the drugs were headed to Mozambique, probably en route to Europe, where they would be worth 131 million on the street; U.S. Drug Enforcement were called in after workers grew suspicious about rice coming in from notorious smuggling zone along the borders of Paraguay, Brazil and Argentina. Thanks Lord for alerting these workers in our other war, meaning the never-ending (it seems) war against drugs in this world of evil perpetrated by the author of evil Satan himself. His goal is to discourage our knowing absolutely our creator God's infinite goodness despite all of these trials we face in this life; it is another "test of faith." "Plane of the Pearls" date in 2007.

244.   Al Qaeda Operative Kashmiri Killed (WPA no. 74)

(04 Jun 11) Saturday: Top Al-Qaeda operative (Ilyas Kashmiri) was killed in a U.S. drone strike, equipped with hell fire missiles, in Pakistan; Kashmiri heads the Al-Qaeda allied Harkat-Ul Jihad Islami (Huji) terror group; official's have labeled him a "specially designated global terrorist"; these facts today generates Pearl 131 and WPA 74 translation lies in "Plane of the Pearls" and thus qualifies as a significant event. Thanks Lord! For eliminating one of the top commanders in this Jihad.

245.   Discovered the Green Book on Coffee Table Matches Size Publisher Desires (6x9)

(05 Jun 11) Sunday: Today is a very special day because it is the feast of "The Ascension of our Lord into Heaven"; as I was pondering this fact sitting on my sofa adjacent to my coffee table I was trying to visualize what the final hard copy of my book would look like; my eyes were fixated on a green book, the "Catechism

of the Catholic Church" in front of me; I was receiving a usual spirit prompt to pick it up and measure its size; my publisher told me the final size would be (6"x9") for the journal (the manuscript was 8 ½ "X 11") when I placed my engineering scale on the green book, mentioned above, it was exactly the same size required by the publisher; what's more it also uses the same format I'm using for my book. VOILA! Holy Spirit power strikes again Pearl 132. Today translated to 2007 falls on a Tuesday. AMEN!

246. Message no. 28 (PROMPT FROM SPIRIT) "Tell My People Your Selected"

(20 Mar 11) (out of seq.) Sunday: I decided to use this important and very significant event flashback and I received my 28th message today at the identical time as (20 Nov 07) recalling my 3rd overwhelming joyful experience that lasted 18 minutes (my longest elapsed time) 2:42 a.m. on the dot. Message no. 28 "Tell my people you are selected and they will believe for I have given you my greatest miracle since I left the world"; I was so filled with joy at that moment I was startled and speechless. Additionally, this date is the feast of the celebration of "The Transfiguration of the Lord" with the apostles on the mountain according to his word, another fact to reflect on; this is the day of 3 (20's) meaning, 2011, 20 Mar 11 and 20 Nov 07; thus three 20's are apparent. Pearl 133 and Pearl 134 are gifted by the Holy Spirit on this magnificent day. Thanks always to my ALMIGHTY FATHER IN HEAVEN. These Pearls today through translation to 2007 fall on Tuesday.

247. Militants (18 Killed) (WPA no. 75)

(07 Jun 11) Tuesday: A U.S. Drone Strike kills 18 militants in North Waziristan Pearl 135 and WPA 75 translation process to 2007 falls on Thursday coinciding with the string equation Y1=70.

248.   Al Qaeda Planner of Attacks Killed (WPA no. 76 and 77)

(11 Jun 11) Saturday: Two significant war events occurred today Pearl 136 and WPA 76-77. As follows: 1) Senior Al-Qaeda planner (Fazul Abdullah Mohammed) wanted for embassy blasts in Tanzania and Kenya 1996 where 2000 U.S. Marines died, was killed in Somalia shootout with government forces. He had a five million dollar bounty on his head. 2) Yemen military killed (21) Al-Qaeda terrorists in the Southern Abyon Province. This pearl lies in the "Plane of the Pearls" when transposed to 2007.

249.   Holy Spirit Received by Apostles "Pentecost" Celebration

(12 Jun 11) Pentecost Sunday: Pearl 137 is gifted today from receiving of the Holy Spirit on this very important date for all mankind conferred on the Apostles of Christ; not only is this a day to remember, but it assures the salvation of our immortal souls.

250.   Migrants Rescued from Trucks in Mexico (CPA no. 76 and 77)

(14 Jun 11) Tuesday: 200 migrants are rescued from suffocating in tractor trailers in Mexico; they paid $3000 each person to human traffickers to reach the U.S.; Pearl 138 and CPA 76 and 77 are realized today. Police seized child exploitation and abuse ring members in worldwide operation. Thanks Lord for answering a very important prayer of mine for bringing these dregs of society to justice. Today is a huge victory for the innocents of our world and coincides with the miracle equation Y1=70, because it falls on a Thursday in 2007.

251.   Representative Gifford's Leaves Hospital "A Walking Miracle" (CPA no. 78 and WPA no. 78)

(16 Jun 11) Thursday: Representative Gabrielle Giffords leaves the hospital after five months following her attempted assassination. Thanks Father for giving her back to us another "walking miracle" from you, just as you did Barbara (Mary's daughter). This definitely constitutes Pearl 139 and CPA 78; because it lies in "The Plane of the Pearls" in regards to my NDE; she was always on my prayer list. Additionally, a war prayer answer also occurred. WPA 78 today when an Iraqi court sentenced 15 alleged Al-Qaeda members to

death for their participation in the 2006 wedding party massacres. The court found the defendants guilty of planning and carrying out the cold blooded murders of 70 innocent people; the attack is viewed by many Iraqi's as one of the most horrific carried out by Sunni-led militants during the insurgency. Thank you Holy Spirit for answering another war time justice Morning Prayer. These two in one day events certainly qualify for meeting the significance test required for a gifted Pearl in "The Plane of the Pearls" of 2007.

252.   "Trinity Sunday" Celebration

(19 Jun 11) Sunday: Two gifted gems Pearl 140 and 141 are apparent today as follows: 1) celebration of Father's day, but especially recognizing this day as "Heavenly Father's" day because our creator God has given all fathers their pro-creation abilities. Today translated back to 2007 falls on Tuesday. 2) Celebration of "Trinity Sunday" with his word given to us as the father=creator, the son= redeemer and finally the Holy Spirit=the love that flows between the Father and the Son; given to the world by creator God as our guide and protector against Satan's temptations.

253.   Militants (12 Killed) in Kurram Area (WPA no. 79)

(21 Jun 11) Tuesday: U.S. Drone strikes in N.W. Pakistan killing at least 12 people. The first strike in Kurram Tribal area targeted a vehicle destroying it and seven occupants. Second strike was a house killing five others. Officials say seven killed were Afghan militants; many Taliban fighters have fled to Kurram, Pakistan to avoid Pakistani Army operations. Pearl 142 and WPA 79 come into focus today. Thanks to Holy Spirit prayer power once again indicating God can eliminate evil at his discretion. Today after taking this from 2011 back to 2007 falls on Thursday. Bingo! Another blue Pearl added to the "String of Pearls."

254.   Leader of Drug Cartel Captured (WPA no. 80) and (CPA no. 79 and 80)

(22 Jun 11) Wednesday: President Calderon of Mexico congratulates his troops for capturing Mendez Vargas. The leader of the La Familia Cartel now extinct. His cartel had plagued Mexico for

years. Pearl 143, WPA 80, and CPA 79 is realized in this morning prayer answer by the Holy Spirit lying in the "Plane of the Pearls" in 2007 translation. Thanks Lord for ending this cartel. Eventually, my most fervent prayer is to win this war on drugs one gang at a time. CPA 80= Boston crime boss James "Whitey Bulger was arrested today in Santa Monica, CA after 16 years on the run. The 81 year old wanted in connection with 19 murders. The former crime boss was arrested alongside his longtime girlfriend and wanted fugitive Catherine Greig. Bulger was listed as no. 2 on the FBI's most wanted list, behind Osama Bin Laden. Arrest was based on a tip from a recent renewed campaign to locate the fugitive criminal. Bulger will appear in Federal Court today. Thanks again Holy Spirit!

255. Insurgents (10 Killed) in Kurram Area (WPA no. 81)

(24 Jun 11) Friday: Today on the Celebration of "The Nativity of St. John the Baptist" Pearl 144 comes into being along with WPA 81 as follows: Pakistani fighter jets killed at
least 10 insurgents after bombing suspected militant hideouts in a Northwestern Region near the Afghan Border; airstrikes hit two areas of the Kurram Tribal region, based on Intel Reports about the presence of militants. We the U.S. have also been launching missile strikes against suspected militants in that region. This Pearl today qualifies as a "Plane of the Pearls" type, because once again it directly links to my NDE of 2007 and all WPA's have to relate to the "War on Terror" only to be automatically on my prayer list. That is the criteria also both events mentioned above are considered significant.

256. Holy Eucharist Feast Day Celebration

(26 Jun 11) Sunday: Pearl 145 arrives on this very important and significant day, the feast of the most Holy Eucharist for Catholics everywhere and other Faith's also can relate to this date given to us by our creator bonding our connection with him forever as we receive his faith shield against the ravages of Satan and other evil spirits who prowl about our world seeking the ruin of souls. Amen! Today translating back to 2007 falls on a Tuesday coinciding with my string of Pearls miracle equation Y1=70.

257. Taliban Commander Killed (WPA no. 82 and 83)

(27 Jun 11) Monday: Pearl 146, WPA 82 and 83. Gunmen kill a Sr. Pakistani Taliban commander who helped train and deploy suicide bombers (Shakirullah Shakir) was gunned down while riding a motorcycle in North Waziristan. Shakir once claimed his group trained more than 1,000 suicide bombers; U.S. drone missile strikes killed 20 militants elsewhere in the region. Thanks Father for those (2) answered war prayers; this pearl was petitioned in my morning prayers months ago; but I am patient when it comes to my prayer list; "Plane of Pearls" date today translated back to 2007.

258. Robbie's Hip Replacement Surgery Successful (CPA no. 81)

(28 Jun 11) Tuesday: My Sister-in-law Robbie had a successful hip replacement today; an answer to my latest morning prayer for her whom I love dearly. Thanks Father for delivering Pearl 147 and CPA 81 for such a wonderful child of yours; of course this date is special and lies implicitly on the string equation Y1=70 on a Thursday in 2007. Thanks again to Holy Spirit prayer power, the very best medicine today.

259. Plotters of Recruit Station Given Life in Prison (WPA no. 84 and 85)

(29 Jun 11) Wednesday: Pearl 148 and WPA 84 and 85 sent today from the Holy Spirit as we celebrate "The Feast of St. Peter the Apostle and St. Paul Apostle/Teacher" acknowledging their importance in God's church. Court hearings took place today for two plotters of terrorism in bringing them to criminal justice; 33 year old Abu Khalid Abdul-Latif and 33 year old Walli Mujahidh were arrested June 22nd after an anti-terror investigation. They're accused of plotting to use machine guns and grenades in an attack at a center that processes U.S. military recruits. They will definitely face life in prison. Additionally, U.S. drone strike kills 50 terrorists in Yemen; our most yet in one attack. Thanks Lord for answering another morning prayer in the war on terror.

260. Message no. 29 (PROMPT FROM SPIRIT) "Blue Pearl Express Train"

(06 Mar 11) (Out of seq.) Sunday: I want to flashback to an all-important Pearl 149 message no. 29, I received as a now familiar prompt from the spirit in the middle of the night as follows: this will be in the form of another analogy. The string equation or straight line is now considered to be analogous to train tracks with the passenger train called "The Blue Pearl Express", the engineer being the Holy Spirit. The destination of this "train" is Heaven via the narrow gate. (see effect no. 1 page 1) I want to reiterate this fact that we, blue pearls, significant events are all aboard and linked together intimately as God's children numbered in the elect. The main goal is for us to remain on this train despite any trials or tribulations God may send our way as a "Test of Faith." We mustn't leave this train at any stopover because it is too difficult for us, for if we do, we'll be selling our souls to the devil and be left behind when this passenger train reaches its destination; eternity with God our creator. Today is one of the most significant events, message no. 29, of this journey through time when translation from 2011 to 2007 forms the mainstay of "The Plane of the Pearls."

261. The Final Revelation for my First Edition

(11 Aug 11) Thursday: Today as I reveal the final post-evidentiary effect Pearl 150, not only is 150 total Pearls realized, but today also coincides with the end of my 80th novena (9 days of prayer each) yielding (80x9) or 720 days of prayer since my NDE. Power combinations math calculation using (R=150) yields 10^{303} power an awesome number. This number is called "centillion" in Webster's Dictionary and demonstrates our creators power for the finale of this journal, how rapidly the total combinations are approaching infinity as its limit (see graphics effect no. 30 page 16) TALK ABOUT REJOICING. WOW!

Conclusion

In the final analysis, it's really up to each reader of this journal to use their intellect and free will to draw their own conclusion; ask yourself, is this, natural cause (caused by nature), or supernatural cause (caused by God) and therefore a miracle? You know my conclusion; REMEMBER FROM PHILOSOPHY, "a man convinced against his will is of the same opinion still"; whatever conclusion you come to I pray that if you and your loved ones will get back to our creator (God) then this journal has met its intended goal. Remember this is the day the LORD has made let all the world rejoice in it and be glad. Hope you enjoyed the journal. I certainly gained much knowledge, love of God and my neighbor with great satisfaction and reward delivering this ultimately important message demonstrating the HOLY SPIRIT's power, showing miracles are being performed today as they were when he was a human being on this earth. Keep the faith and your loved ones close to you and let them know how much you care for them every day of their lives, because as I discovered how quickly in an instant of time, this life on earth can vanish because it is temporal and our immortal soul will pass on to eternity with our HEAVENLY FATHER. AMEN! Thank you for sharing my near-death experience with you. May the good Lord bless all of you for listening to this message given to me by HIS Holy Spirit. AMEN! Heed these words and spread this good news throughout the world today and remember what God himself said, "if you do not acknowledge me before man I will not acknowledge you and accept you for my kingdom which is in heaven." Look for a forthcoming sequel or second edition of my journal, if the HOLY SPIRIT continues to bless me by gifting additional "PEARLS."